Jean Malou

On the choice of a state of life

Jean Malou

On the choice of a state of life

ISBN/EAN: 9783337202330

Printed in Europe, USA, Canada, Australia, Japan

Cover: Foto ©Andreas Hilbeck / pixelio.de

More available books at **www.hansebooks.com**

ON

THE CHOICE

OF

A STATE OF LIFE.

BY THE LATE BISHOP OF BRUGES.

Translated from the French by

ALOYSIUS DEL VITTORIO.

WITH A PREFACE

BY

THE BISHOP OF SALFORD.

LONDON:

BURNS & OATES, 17 & 18, PORTMAN STREET, W.

AND 63, PATERNOSTER ROW, E.C.

1874.

TO THE

RECTOR,

PROFESSORS AND STUDENTS

OF

ST. JOSEPH'S MISSIONARY COLLEGE,

MILL HILL, LONDON,

WHOSE ZEAL I ADMIRE,

WHOSE FRIENDSHIP I ESTEEM,

AND

FOR WHOSE HOSPITALITY I AM GRATEFUL :

This Translation

IS,

BY KIND PERMISSION,

DEDICATED.

A. D. V.

PREFACE.

THE subject treated on in this little volume is
one of vital interest, not perhaps of direct interest
to every one, but to a large and increasing class.
It is not to every person that God offers the choice
of a state of life. For there are many before
whose view He opens out but one path, and they
find themselves upon it of necessity and without
choice. They are thus freed from all responsibility
and perplexity in ascertaining the Divine will.
Their Heavenly Father has Himself put them
down upon the road they should travel. But there
are others to whom He offers a choice. He knows,
indeed, the precise position of life in which He
would have them serve Him. His graces await
them, and all is prepared along their path just
as preparations are made along a road upon which
a prince is presently expected to pass. But to
ascertain the Divine will is often an affair of
great difficulty. Our Lord is pleased to try and
prove us, in order to inspire us with a greater distrust in ourselves and a great confidence in Him.
He forces us to pray and to practise many virtues
before the ship is allowed to weigh anchor, and

to make out of port for the high and open sea.
When a youth makes his final choice of a state
of life, he knows that he is staking his happiness
in this world and the next upon that act. No
wonder, then, that it should be called a vital question. It is also the turning point between childhood
and the responsibility of manhood.

Three things are needful, in order to ascertain
our vocation when in doubt about it: prayer,
reflection, and wise counsel. If we faithfully use
these means we shall obtain peace and certainty.
Though the avenues to the various paths of life
be ever so dark to him who has not traversed
them, and though the ways of God be ever so
hidden and mysterious, the dawn will come. For
"*qui fecit ex tenebris lucem splendescere, Ipse
illuxit in cordibus nostris.*" God Himself is the
Morning Star arising upon high to visit those who
hope in Him: "*Post tenebras spero lucem.*" The
Church teaches us to cry to Him, as to the Light
itself :—

> O Lux beatissima,
> Reple cordis intima
> Tuorum fidelium.

With prayer must be joined serious reflection.
"*In meditatione mea exardescit ignis.*" If a
person called to the ecclesiastical or religious
state does not from the beginning intellectually

master his position; if he does not carefully survey its breadth, its responsibilities, and its excellence, he will fall short—first, in his aim, and then in the attainment even of that aim. " *Intellectus cogitabundus principium omnis boni*" is eminently true in this early stage, when choosing a state of life. The special value of the accompanying treatise by the late Bishop of Bruges is that it sets the mind thinking. It raises a high estimate of the importance of the choice to be made, and points out many of the characteristics of a true vocation. But in addition to this, as food for reflection, I would strongly advise every one who is examining his or her vocation to read the " Lives of the Saints ;" not those short lives, which are little better than a synopsis, but the fuller biographies. These introduce us to an intimate acquaintance with the saints, who are the only true heroes and heroines the world has ever seen ; they are also the encouraging models set up before us by our Blessed Lord. It is therefore useful to have their example before our eyes when examining our vocation. Lastly, to prayer and reflection should be added consultation with a prudent director. It is his business to correct mistakes which persons easily fall into about themselves, and to ascertain the impulse and guidance of the Holy Spirit. This is the ordinary way of God's providence. He sent

Saul to Ananias in order that he might learn with certainty the nature of his vocation.

It may not here be out of place to say a few words to parents and guardians as to their duty in the matter of the vocation of their children. First, they have no right to take the settlement of the state of life of their children into their own hands· Vocation comes from God, and not from parents He who has numbered the hairs of our head, and does not permit even a sparrow to fall to the ground without His knowledge and concurrence, has determined the place and the occupation during life of each one of His children. He leads without forcing, suggests without constraining, and addresses Himself to the reason and the will, so that in the matter of vocation we may truly say to Him with the wise man, " *Cum magna reverentia disponsis nos* " (Wisd. xiii. 18). Again, nothing is dearer to God than the Mystical Body of Christ, which is being formed and built up until it shall be completed. Each one of us is destined to be a member of that Body: " but all the members have not the same office." " Different gifts " are assigned to each. " Every one hath his proper gift from God; one after this manner and another after that." " To one He gave five talents, and to another two, and to another one : to everyone according to his proper ability." St. Paul, teaching the faithful of Corinth, says distinctly, "As *God* hath called every one so let him walk; and so I teach in all the churches. Let every man abide in the same calling in which he was called."

Lastly. God having provided abundant graces for each one in the path into which He calls him, it would be the height of cruelty on the part of parents if, for their own personal gratification or for some imaginary benefit, they were to deprive their children of these graces and of their fruits both in this life and the next. The parent may experience a brief joy in retaining his child or in constraining his course; but it will be a short-lived pleasure, and must end in sorrow and regrets. Catholic doctrine upon this subject is very clear. St. Alphonsus in his Moral Theology (*lib.* iv. n. 77) teaches that " it must be held with the common opinion of theologians that parents are guilty of mortal sin who, by threatening, or frightening, or deceiving their children, or by imploring them and holding out promises to them, seek to induce them to give up their vocation." He says that they are guilty of two sins: the one against charity for the reason which is obvious, and the other against parental piety, for they are bound *sub gravi* to educate their children and to attend to their spiritual welfare. He adds, however, that home. It is perfectly true that where a child is absolutely necessary to the life or livelihood of a parent, filial piety bars the vocation, at least for the time being. But a mere sentimental necessity, strong and passionate feelings, and even the great convenience and value of the child's services at home, are not sufficient motives to warrant a parent in refusing consent when it seems otherwise clear that God is calling the soul to serve Him in another state of life. If, under these circumstances, the parent refuse consent, the child has a right, and often an imperative duty, to follow the vocation of God without the consolation of the parental approval: "We must obey God rather than man."

It sometimes happens that the signs of a vocation, which are said to be *aptitude* and *attraction* for a state, are completely over-ruled by the interests of God's glory. Nothing practically can be better or more meritorious than to order one's life "*ad majorem Dei gloriam*," whether this lead us to embrace a "state" which is lower in itself or not. It is not the excellence of the "state" considered in itself that a soul should regard; but the greater honour and glory of our Divine Master should absorb its whole attention. He who looks first to the glory of his Master will be provided for beyond all others. Thus the famous Countess Matilda sought to abandon the world and to enter a convent, there to devote herself to a life of pure contemplation and prayer. But St. Gregory, hearing of her desire, interposed and forbade her to carry it into execution. He knew that she could render greater service to God and His Church by the use of her influence and power in the world than by embracing the higher state of life to which she aspired. And so it may happen from time to time that God's glory will require that men and women should remain in the world, whose *aptitude* and *attraction* are for the religious or ecclesiastical state. But decision in this matter demands great prudence, and should be come to only when confirmed by the counsel of a truly enlightened and spiritual person. The advice which is often tendered by those good but worldly persons, whose judgments are swayed by human motives and governed by human prudence, should be treated with the greatest suspicion

I must not omit to make mention here of a remarkable example of the way in which vocations to the religious state, so far as they are indicated by " aptitude and attraction," may be set aside by positive laws of the Church. Thus both the Constitutions of the Pontifical Colleges and the missionary oath which the canon law requires of all priests ordained in England and elsewhere *ad titulum missionis*, impose a grave obligation not to enter a religious order or congregation. And yet the "state" of a priest who is also a religious is higher and holier in itself than that of a priest who is not a religious; for the religious has contracted an obligation to observe three of the Evangelical Counsels of Perfection in perpetuity, whereas the simple priest has not. One of the oldest colleges. in Rome is the German College. Its first constitutions were drawn up by St. Ignatius himself, and they were confirmed in a bull by Pope Gregory XIII., beginning, "*Ex Collegio Germanico.*" This bull prescribes the very form of oath to be taken by each student after he has been six months in the college, and it obliges him to accept and observe the superior's interpretation of the rules, to take Orders when called, to serve the Mission in Germany, and never to enter any religious order or congregation. There were not wanting persons who, in their zeal for the religious state, dared to criticise the Pope and to attack the oath, saying that it was opposed to the glory of God and to the spiritual welfare of those who took it. But the learned Father Cordara, in his commentary upon the rule and constitutions of this celebrated college, undertook its defence. " If you look closely into the matter," he says, "you

will clearly see that, although all religious insti-
tutes are more holy than any other state whatsoever
beneath that of the episcopacy, they are not more
useful to others and to society. Society certainly is
more benefited by him who, after the example of
the apostles, devotes himself wholly to the salvation of his fellow men, than by him who shuts
himself up in certain enclosures to attend to
himself alone and his own salvation. Moreover, the
constitution of this college does not look to the
private sanctification of its students so much as to
the public good of the people : and Pope Gregory's
design was not to train up within its walls
simply a body of holy men, but a body of priests
who should be thoroughly apostolic men." And
therefore (he continues) it was quite just and
proper to put obstacles in the way of their entering
religion, more especially when he who raises the
obstacles has the power, when he thinks fit, to
remove them.

It may be worth while to add a few words of
explanation on the missionary oath taken in this
country. For it sometimes happens that very
pious, but perhaps not very wise or well in-
structed, persons profess to be shocked when
priests who have been ordained *ad titulum missionis*
seek to join a religious order and are finally
hindered from doing so by their oath. The

instruction issued by the *Sacred Congregation de Propaganda Fide,* April 27, 1871, describes the men thus ordained as those " *qui in arduum apostolici ministerii opus assumuntur,*" and it says that, " like the students of the Pontifical Colleges, they are bound to take an oath, by which they swear to give themselves up for life to labour in the mission to which they have been or shall be appointed ;" and it adds that " the Holy See has regularly exacted this oath in order to provide for the spiritual good of those missions which educate their clergy ;" and that dispensation from it, in order to enter religion, can be obtained from the Holy See alone, which reserves to itself, after hearing the Ordinary, the decision as to whether the necessities of the mission would justify it. " For (continues the Instruction) public must take precedence of private interests, on the same principle that the members of certain religious orders are not allowed by the Church to join a stricter Order without the permission of their own superiors."

In other words, the Church legislates for the greater glory of God and the salvation of souls. We cannot propose a higher motive to ourselves than this, and to submit to her wise legislation is a high road to sanctity. At the same time I am far from saying that priests who have taken

A*

the missionary oath are not sometimes called by God to the religious state.

Strong and irresistible impulses from God towards the religious state, or the conviction that for him personally salvation can . be attained only in that state, are reasons which entirely justify, and indeed compel, a priest to seek for a dispensation from his oath. But it must also be borne in mind that the Holy See is fully justified in refusing the dispensation, as she frequently does, and that her refusal may be taken as an authoritative declaration, in the face of private impulses and personal feeling, that there is in the particular case no Divine vocation to the religious state.

The question then may naturally arise, Are they who, without any fault on their own part, are deprived of the opportunity of entering a religious order, thereby deprived of the means of attaining that spiritual perfection of which the highest pattern is set before us in the Gospel? Or, to make the question and answer more comprehensive, Are those persons who are not called to a religious order, but serve God as simple priests or laymen in the world, unable to lead a life of evangelical perfection? Note in the first place that in the kingdom of God there are "diversities of graces," "diversities of ministeries," and "diversities of operations, but the same God, who worketh in all. And the manifestation of the spirit is given to every man unto profit ". (1 Cor.xii. 6, 7). In this manner, indeed, the different states of life have excellencies and perfections each their own, while the Gospel is the rule and standard of them all. The sanctity and perfection of the soul consist in charity. Charity itself is dependent first on the observance of the Commandments, and then on the practice of counsels. No man can attain to the perfection of charity who does not practise some, at least, of the counsels of the Gospel. There are many counsels of perfection. The frequent and fervent reception of the Sacraments is a counsel of perfection, and one of the principal means of attaining perfection—Confession producing purity of soul, and Holy Communion a closer union between the soul and His Divine majesty. The greater degree of fervour with which the Commandments are observed; the more intense purity of intention we cultivate; the turning the left check to the striker who has smitten us on the right; the choosing the lowest place; the giving of large alms or all we possess; the spending long hours in prayer; the mortification of our body by fasting, and many other acts of virtue are counsels of the Gospel and of perfection. But among all the counsels there are three which are called emphatically "the Evangelical Counsels." The profession and practice of these three Evangelical Counsels—Voluntary Poverty, Perpetual Chastity and Entire Obedience—are of the essence of a religious order. No religious order can exist without them: and their members have the great additional profit, merit and blessing of binding themselves to their observance for life. But, like prayer and fasting and the frequentation of the Sacraments, these counsels are means and instruments towards the attainment of perfection, not perfection itself: They are indeed most peculiarly efficacious means, practised by our Blessed Lord Himself, and inculcated by word and example upon His disciples (Matt. c. 19). Note in the second place that they are not the exclusive property of religious orders. The life of perfection which they foster and develope was long antecedent to the formation of those religious associations which we call the religious orders. The Evangelical Counsels were of Divine institution, and were practised and spread among the early Christians by the apostles and their immediate successors in the cure of souls. The religious orders arose after the Church had been forming and perfecting her saints for centuries upon the Gospel pattern of perfection. Bishops and priests, martyrs, confessors and virgins had lived in the world for hundreds of years, faithful as the apostles themselves had been to the observance of the Evangelical Counsels.

When the religious orders arose they did but gather together and organize the elements which already existed; they made public and solemn profession of a life which had been lovingly embraced with less of formality and publicity by all who had aspired to the perfection of the Gospel from the days of the apostles; they raised up walls around enclosures into which those who desired to practise the counsels apart from the world and free from its temptations and allurements might withdraw. The practice of the counsels was always exposed to decay under the corroding and disintegrating influence of the atmosphere of the world. The tendency of human nature to laxity and indulgence augmented the danger in the presence of an adverse public opinion and practice. The religious orders therefore conferred an incalculable benefit on mankind by opening out peaceful retreats and shelters from the world for the practice of the counsels of perfection; by the creation of a public opinion of their own, and by the rules and constitutions which perpetually bound their members together in the pursuit of perfection. They became the examples, witnesses, heralds and preachers of the Evangelical Counsels. They are exclusive in their character, because they exclude from their society all who do not bind themselves to " the three counsels" of perfection. But they are not exhaustive of evangelical perfection in the Church, they claim no monopoly of the counsels, they do not profess to drain the world, still less the priesthood, of every soul that is called by God to the practice of the Gospel counsels. They abound themselves, but they desire that all should abound.

Unfortunately a different view has gained admittance in some quarters, which has been most disastrous in its effects, not only upon thousands of persons living in the world, but also upon some of the priesthood. And perhaps the very minute and analytical discussion of the question of vocation, laying greater stress upon the differences than upon the similarities and points in common between different states of life, has somewhat tended to favour and strengthen this view, which starts with a strong alliance upon its side, namely, that of the weakness of human nature and its proclivity to ease and indulgence. Thus, to put it broadly, it is sometimes said that the Evangelical Counsels of perfection, which the Church teaches us to hold in the highest esteem, belong to the religious orders, and that no one should attempt to practise them unless he or she is prepared to enter an Order.

Indeed, it not unfrequently happens that persons

living in the world are made the subject of unsparing criticism because they are known to practise some or all of the Evangelical Counsels: they are reproached for being unlike the world, dressing in black; wearing poor apparel; practising poverty in their personal habits; shunning pleasure parties; ignoring the fashions—as though these did not govern society—and living under obedience to a rule of life and to a director. Such persons, it is said, are fit only for the cloister: they should be labelled and ticketed off with a religious habit. But the persons who utter these reproaches can be excused from downright worldliness only upon the plea of downright ignorance of the spirit of the Gospel and of the history of the Church from the beginning. The life and writings of St. Jerome and of St. Ambrose and their companions and disciples are evidence of how the counsels of perfection may be practised in private families and in the midst of the world. And every age of the Church has furnished similar evidence. It is no answer to say that the Orders and Congregations have become so numerous and represent so large a variety of work and attraction, that all who follow the counsels should be transplanted out of this busy or fashionable world into their sacred precincts. There are many persons in the world who are simply unable to become religious. Sometimes it is duty, sometimes health, or age, sometimes poverty that keeps them in the world and closes against them the doors of the Orders. At other times it may be the clear apprehension that God does not call them to a community life, and that they can serve Him best by turning their opportunities in the world to His honour and service.

To many of these persons is opened by our Lord the wide field of the Gospel counsels. Voluntary poverty, perpetual mortification and self-denial, and obedience to rule and direction may be their surest way to perfection. We possess, thanks be to God, thousands of holy persons in the world, men and women, married and single, among the poor more than among the rich, whose lives are spent in the constant practice of some of the Evangelical Counsels of perfection. The schools they support, the churches they build and maintain, their gifts to God at the altar, their alms to the poor, imply the practice, not of the ordinary virtue of charity, but of the Counsel of Voluntary poverty in a high degree. They bare themselves of their earnings and of all they possess, except that which is needful for their scanty subsistence, and entrench even upon this in order that, living in the world, they may have lot and honour with the early Christians in the poverty and charity of Christ.

Again, there is the case of ecclesiastical students

in our colleges and seminaries, and of some of
our diocesan clergy. They may have no vocation
to a religious order, or having a desire to enter one,
prior obligations may interfere and bar their way.
Yet they may have an ardent desire of perfection
and may thirst after the practice of the Evangelical
Counsels. May not they adopt these counsels as
their own? May they not live upon them, and
practise them in all their detail, without being
considered eccentric and wanting in judgment and
Christian sense? Assuredly they may. In the
first place, the counsel of Chastity, with all its
restraints and precautions, is binding upon them;
and about this no more need be said. Next, beyond
the practice of the ordinary virtue of obedience
to the Church, which is due even from the laity, the
ecclesiastic enters into a voluntary and lasting
engagement, by his mission oath, and again in his
ordination, to obey his bishop. He becomes subject
to the general ecclesiastical canons, and to the
decrees and regulations for life and discipline, which
may be laid upon him by his bishop in visitation
and extra-synodically as well as in synod. He has
thus a rule of life and conduct prescribed for him
which he is bound to follow. His renunciation
of self will and his obedience are so far complete.
He has ceased to be his own master. His life is
consecrated by the strength of a triple obligation to

the service of God and of souls. He is bound by the very nature and end of his priesthood—"*nemo sibi pontifex;*" he is bound by the solemn promise made to his bishop at ordination; and he is bound, moreover, if ordained under the privilege granted to the clergy in this missionary country, by a sacred vow and oath, from which none but the highest authority on earth can release him, to labour for the salvation of souls. This vow, like the vows of religion, is perpetual, and its duties press upon him as long as he has health and life to discharge them. The following are the words which he pronounces:—*Voveo pariter et juro, quod in hac Diœcesi perpetuo in divinis administrandis laborem meum et operam, sub omnimoda directione et jurisdictione R.P.D., pro tempore Ordinarii, pro salute animarum impendam.*

Lastly, with regard to the counsel of Voluntary Poverty, the secular priest is free to embrace it, and he may practise it with all the fidelity observed by religious living on the mission. He is under no obligation; he is free. He is not bound to make this particular counsel the special object of his predilection; but many reasons may lead him to do so; and he may bind himself if he please, even by vow, to spend nothing upon himself, upon creature comforts, upon food or furniture, upon amusements and pleasures, beyond that which is absolutely necessary; absolutely necessary, that is, for the proper discharge of his duties. A priest upon the English mission who sets himself to consider in what way he can practise the counsel of Voluntary Poverty will find a thousand opportunities at his hand in daily life. We are nationally and constitutionally as a people prone to spend. No race is less thrifty in personal expenditure. But that which pastors lose by extravagance or want of care is lost to the poor, to the Church and to Christ. To economise in details, to pinch and save for the purpose of hoarding, is to engender the spirit of the miser; and the apostle admonishes us in his instruction to Timothy that "the desire of money is the root of all evils" (1 Tim. vi. 10). But when savings are effected, and self-denial is practised from the spirit of holy poverty, the money thus collected is given over to the poor or to the Church. The poverty of the Gospel is golden, but the poverty of the world is dross.

The diocesan clergy of this country are placed, for the most part, in circumstances which greatly facilitate the practice among them of evangelical poverty. Churches and schools are carried on upon a strain; new spiritual wants are continually arising, and their supply is dependent upon alms as a basis; fresh missions have to be opened, and the calls from all sides upon the priest are

perpetual.   They who possess something of their
own are being continually invited to spend it;
they who have but a little are being ever incited
to divide even that little, and the less each one
retains of his own the more he is reminded of
the poverty of our Lord, which Lallement calls "*the
foundation of the apostolic life.*"   "Having food
and wherewith to be covered, with these we are
content;" such was the simple teaching of St.
Paul when forming the character and mind of the
Christian priesthood.

St. Charles, who is the model of the diocesan
priesthood, used not unfrequently to remind his
clergy of this virtue of poverty, which he practised so rigorously in his own person.   On one
occasion, speaking to his priests, he asked them,
"Do you know how great is the perfection of
complete poverty?—how great and valuable the
assistance which it renders to fishers of souls?—
how strictly the Lord required its observance in
those first fishermen, the apostles, whom He permitted to 'carry neither purse, nor scrip, nor
shoes?'" (Hom. cxx.)   And elsewhere he said:
"Take as your pattern the lives of the holy fathers
of old; after the example of the saints, live in
such poverty, that what you may have to give
for your churches and the adornment of your altars
and other sacred objects may not be merely the

overflow of your superfluity, but rather savings
stolen by mortification from your necessary maintenance."

Finally, the thought of this noble Christian
virtue of poverty, adopted by the Lord as a spouse,
not only reconciles many a hard-working, humble
diocesan priest to his necessary poverty, but it
sweetens his privations, while it fills his mind with
peace and content. And if the thought should
arise that in his old age or sickness the doors of no
well provided community or home will be opened
to receive him, and that he can look forward to
none but a scanty allowance upon which to eke out
his remnant of life, so far from being dejected, he
will rejoice the more, in the poverty of Him
who "being rich became poor for our sake," and
will comfort himself with the assurance of the
prophet, "*Ego egenus et pauper sum, Dominus
sollicitus est mei.*"

I have dwelt somewhat at length upon the practice of the Evangelical Counsels, which are so
closely connected with a life of perfection, because
this little volume is destined to fall into the hands
of many persons who have no vocation to the
religious state. And it is they rather than those
who are called to one or other of the Orders who
need to be reminded that the Gospel counsels
were addressed by our Lord to "the disciples"

and to "the multitude," with the notice to all
men; "*qui potest capere capiat.*" It is an unprofitable and foolish thing to compare the merits
of one saint with those of another, and it is not
wise to draw comparisons between different Orders,
and between one holy state of life and another,
measuring them, as it were, one against another.
Each and all have their proper excellence and
perfection, with their pre-determined place in the
Body of Christ.   Let every youth, therefore, by
prayer, examination and counsel, ascertain the
state to which he is called by God, and having
found it, let him fix his mind and heart upon it:
let him study its special spiritual characteristics,
and let him make them his own.   We must
reverence and esteem all the states and Orders in
the Church, but we are bound especially to love
and cherish our own.

✠ HERBERT, Bishop of Salford.

Salford September 8, 1874.

PREFACE.

THIS is a translation from the second edition of Mgr. Malou's excellent book, *Règles pour le Choix d'un état de Vie*, and will, it is hoped, supply a want which undoubtedly exists in our literature, that, namely, of a scientific and practical treatise on vocations. The late Bishop of Bruges is well known on the Continent as the author of several such works, whose value depends not only upon the learning and piety of their writer, but also upon his great practical experience in the work of the ministry and in the training of youth. And what period of life needs so much a good and trusty adviser as that critical moment when a person's future career has to be decided upon, and this especially when there is question between the Church or the world? It is indeed the crisis, the Rubicon of a lifetime : a person's happiness for this world and the next is hanging in the scales. In this momentous and anxious period, the calm and thoroughly practical counsels and directions of our author will, we hope, serve as a sure chart and trustworthy guide. To be the means of introducing such a guide to even one or two who lack his aid, would be indeed a great and sufficient reward for all our labours.

The quotations in the French edition are, unfortunately, often very inexact. All those from Holy Scripture I have carefully verified, and in all cases quoted the authorized Douay version. I am sorry that, writing at a distance from any great library, I have been unable to do the same for the various quotations from the fathers and ecclesiastical writers. However, I have to acknowledge the kindness of a friend in St. Cuthbert's College, Ushaw, who has verified a few such for me in the library of that institution.

No further liberty has been taken with the text than the omitting of a few sentences which were written especially with reference to Belgium, and which, therefore, would have no value to an English reader.

January 17, 1874.

SKETCH OF THE LIFE OF MGR. MALOU,

BISHOP OF BRUGES.

———

It will not be inappropriate to append to this Preface a few words upon the life of the pious and learned author whose work is now offered to English youth ; inasmuch as that life is in itself a perfect model for our young men, and especially for such as this book is particularly addressed to.

John Baptist Malou was a native of Ypres. Born of a good family on June 30th, 1809, his distinguished qualities of heart and mind marked him out even as a boy for an eminent career, and at the age of eleven he was sent to France, where he entered the famous Jesuit College of St. Acheul, near Amiens. Here he remained until the suppression of the college by a decree of Charles X. in 1828, passing through a more than ordinarily brilliant course of humanities and philosophy. But, side by side with his extraordinary talents, he had developed the still rarer qualities of the soul, and young as he was, he was already looked up to by his comrades as a model and a guide. His advice and his guidance were constantly sought for by them ; and the confidence which was placed in them at that early period may be taken for a sure

A**

warrant of the value of the same when offered at a more mature age to all Christian youth in the present little treatise : for is it not said that school-fellows are generally found to be the best judges of character and parts ?

Though only nineteen when he left St. Acheul, his name was already surrounded by the highest *éclat* of academical success. But at this point he met with an unexpected obstacle, for the government of his native country—Belgium—had, in a fit of folly, closed the doors of the colleges to all who had studied in foreign parts. The result was that young Malou was detained for three years in apparent idleness at home. We say *apparent*, because after all he was making headway all this time, and these three years were probably more valuable to him in the long run than they would have been had things taken their ordinary course. In the first place, he had a full opportunity of trying all the world could offer. He made his entrance into society, and whilst his talents and acquirements helped to make him shine therein, he also had opportunities of improving himself in general culture and refinement. Moreover, he employed his leisure in devoting himself to a course of mathematical studies. But, above all, he turned his time to good account by constant prayer. The outcome of all was that he felt decidedly called to leave the world and prepare still more definitely for the levitical life. But his resolution was not taken on a sudden. Faithful to that advice which he strives to impress upon his readers in the present treatise, he determined to " go apart " in order to make a full deliberation. The place he chose was at the Apostles' tomb, and in June, 1831, he went to Rome. He had here the benefit of the advice of many master of the spiritual life, and especially of the Cardinal Prince Charles Odescalchi, the illustrious Bishop of Sabina, and Papal Vicar, whose edifying humiliation and saintly death he touchingly alludes to in the latter part of this book. The result was that with three compatriots, all destined to be bishops in the same hierarchy, he entered the ecclesiastical *Collegio Nobile*, whence he passed to the famous German College, probably the most brilliant and successful of the Roman colleges. His academical career reopened with its wonted *éclat;* and in 1835 he obtained the doctor's cap with great renown. His studies over, he hastened to return to his diocese in order to begin work.

Fortunately his Bishop, Mgr. Boussen, could recognize and appreciate the invaluable qualities of the young priest, so pious and so learned. Nor did his fame stop here, for two years later an event occurred which showed how widespread was his reputation. The Belgian Catholic hierarchy founded the Catholic University at Mechlin in 1834, and in 1836 transferred it to Louvain, the beginning of a great and glorious career destined to rival that of the great universities of the Middle Ages. Hardly was it established in its new home, when the young

Father Malou—he was only 28 years of age—was nominated Professor of Dogmatic Theology. He held this chair for eleven years with more than ordinary distinction. A young man of weaker soul, an Abailard, would have been puffed up and ruined by this extraordinary elevation. It was not so with Dr. Malou. If he had the talents of a St. Bernard, he had also his humility. Nothing is more remarkable at this time than his industry. *The more you have to do, the more time you will find to do it in,* is the maxim of a thoughtful writer, which is borne out by every one's daily experience. The young professor, devoting himself with zeal to the work of his chair, occupied himself in a profound study of theology, and yet found time to act as librarian, to deliver religious conferences to the students, to undertake the duties of a confessor, and to give himself to an enormous course of reading. We are told that he "devoured" books in every branch of literature, and that his reading was so far from being superficial, that he wrote critical remarks upon most of the books he read. At this time, also, he produced his first specimens of original writing, and these soon made him known to the theologians of the Catholic world.

It is no wonder, then, that his venerable bishop, feeling his strength fail and his end approach, should fix his eyes upon Dr. Malou as his coadjutor and future successor. In 1847, Mgr. Boussen, with the concurrence of his Chapter, made the request for this appointment to the Holy See; but before

it could be granted the venerable prelate died
and Pius IX. in his exile at Gaëta signed the bull
nominating Dr. Malou, not to the coadjutorship,
but to the Bishopric of Bruges, at the close of
1848.

. We shall say little or nothing of his glorious
episcopacy of fifteen years. One sentence alone
will suffice to sum it all up, and it is this: *The
zeal of Thy House hath eaten me up.* What particularly concerns us and our readers is his intense
interest in the education and direction of youth.
Schools of all classes for the theologian and for
the child he established, renovated or reorganized
throughout his diocese; and his efforts to give
an impetus to studies of all sorts met with decided
success. He held "pedagogic conferences" of the
directors and masters, in order to discuss their
programmes of study and discipline. Better still,
he instituted annual competitive examinations between scholar and scholar, and between school and
school.

But it was his young ecclesiastics who were the
dearest objects of his cares. Any one reading the
present work will not fail to see the interest he
took in them, and the peculiar capacity he had for
training them. We are not surprised, therefore, at
his success. He has himself left the statement in
writing that it had been his constant prayer to
Heaven that he might never ordain a young ecclesiastic who had no vocation, or who was one day
to dishonour it. "I think," he adds, "that Heaven

has granted me this favour. There is only one of whom I feel any doubt: and that one is enough to force from me daily bitter tears, and to make me constantly fear the judgment of God." (In a M.S. entitled, *Conseils à Mon Successeur*.)

This model prelate died in 1864, the victim of a disease which had for years been his constant and cruel companion. The funeral oration was pronounced, in his Cathedral Church of Bruges, by Mgr. de Montpellier, Bishop of Liège, his fellow-student and colleague in the episcopacy; and to this affectionate eulogium * we are indebted for the present brief sketch.

May this translation help some one young Catholic at least to follow in its author's footsteps.

Transfiguration Sunday, 1874.

* Oraison Funèbre, Bruxelles, 1864.

INTRODUCTION.

GOD, who is the Beginning and the End of all things, has not only fixed the grades of the angelic hierarchy in the highest heavens, and dictated the laws which, in this universe, direct the course of visible nature; He has also created the moral world, the kingdom of His Son, the spiritual family which is preparing itself here below to reign one day in heaven.

If he assigns to the angels their mission on earth, to the stars their orbit in space, we cannot doubt that He marks out for man, too, the career which he must follow, in order to please his God and arrive at his own happiness. God cannot be indifferent to the individual direction of souls, nor a stranger to the choice of states of life. If there exist in the world a creature capable of disarranging or of seconding the plans of His providence, that creature is, without doubt, *man*, who, endowed with reason, armed with free will, placed betwixt the true and the false, betwixt good and evil, can obey Him or resist Him; and, according to the measure of his fidelity or his opposition, can become for the whole of God's people either a subject of edification or a stone of stumbling.

Now, it is certain that the good or bad behaviour of men depends almost entirely upon the state they have embraced. If that state is the one assigned them by Providence as the most suited to their character, their strength, and even their weaknesses, we may assert, as a general rule, that they will behave themselves well. If, on the contrary, they embrace, through outward attraction, passion or thoughtlessness, a state to which God does not call them, or which He forbids them, their behaviour will be blameworthy and evil. This is the idea of St. Gregory of Nazianzus :—"For my part," he says, "I maintain that the choice of a state of life is so important, as to decide, for the rest of our existence, the goodness or badness of our behaviour." Thus the choice of a state of life resembles, in certain respects, vocation to the faith, or even predestination; it decides for us a whole course of duties to be fulfilled; a long series of graces to be obtained—graces like to a chain, which binds us to heaven and draws us thitherward. If we grasp this chain, we are saved; if we let it go, we are lost.

We must, then, avoid the idea that the choice of a state of life is an indifferent matter, in

which we may follow, without any ill result, our
taste or our whims. God claims *His* rights in
it ; He demands to be a party to it, and very
often to subject it to His will. He has particular
views concerning each one of us. If He destines
the greater part of men to an ordinary life, He,.
nevertheless, reserves to Himself the choice of
the leaders of His people and of those individuals
whom He wishes to employ in the world as the
instruments of His mercy or His justice. One
He destines to serve the Church in the ecclesiastical state ; another to edify God's people by
the practice of the evangelical counsels and of
the perfect life ; a third to be a bright, shining
light in the world by the brilliancy of Christian
virtues, and to be a useful servant of the State.
It belongs not to us to reverse these parts, to
exchange these careers. A young man, called to
the priesthood or the cloister, will not save himself
by life in the world ; another, called to life in
the world, will be lost if he engage himself in
the cloister or the priesthood.

In the matter of vocation to a state of life, we
cannot make a mistake with impunity; we are culp-
able if we resist the voice of Heaven; we are equally
so if we deafen ourselves so as to be unable to
hear it.

It is of highest importance, therefore, to procced in this matter with thoughtfulness, with a full knowledge of the case, and, above all, with a disposition of perfect submission to God's will.

The great difficulty in this matter arises almost always from the inexperience of those who deliberate about it, and from the shifting nature of their affections. When young people first begin to gaze steadily and seriously upon the future, a thousand different ideas—sometimes contradictory ones—in turn take possession of their minds, and hurry them on into the greatest perplexity. At one time the future appears to them all radiant, clear and brilliant; at another, it appears uncertain, lowering, threatening. On one side the world spreads out its riches, dignities and pleasures; on the other, our Divine Saviour, Jesus Christ, shows Himself with His Cross and His Gospel, and seems to say: "If you wish to be happy, follow me!" Vice appears, on the one hand, supported by her *prestige* and her seductive attraction: virtue, on the other, with her charming simplicity, her heavenly sweetness, her deathless rewards. Sometimes the mind can only see feeble glimmerings, at others it meets with nothing but gloom and darkness; at others, again, its eyes are dazzled with the brightest lights: and so the soul struggles in painful alternations of fear and hope, sadness and joy. Earthly affections clash in the heart's core with Divine attractions, and these opposite motions appear to lead only to doubt and uncertainty. This position is a painful one, we must acknowledge; it would appear unbearable if it were to be continued for a long time. But a young Christian comes forth from it without difficulty the moment he lifts up his thoughts and his hand towards heaven to invoke the Father of Lights—the moment he asks counsel of his Mother, the Church, and yields himself up to the sovereign decrees of Providence. God then procures for him, as heretofore for St. Paul, an Ananias to enlighten him, to guide him, to lead him by the hand along easy paths to a definite determination, whence springs that sense of conviction and that calm that afterwards forms his entire happiness.

But to come to land in the harbour, we must consult the compass, handle the rudder, unfurl the sails: I mean we must manage this business with great sentiments of faith, humility and fervour.

It is in order to facilitate this examination for Christian youth—so dear to us—that we have compiled these pages, in which we shall not speak of ourselves; all that we shall say we have heard from the Divine oracles of the Holy Spirit; we have learnt from the holy fathers, our teachers in virtue as in faith; or we have drawn from the lessons of a long experience.

May these few pages, which have been inspired to us by our love of youth, enlighten, console, strengthen, encourage the faithful who are deliberating about the choice of a state of life; and so contribute to the glory of God and to the joy of our Holy Mother the Church!

RULES FOR THE

CHOICE OF A STATE OF LIFE.

CHAPTER I.

Of the Nature of a State of Life, and of the Number of States of Life.

WE must first of all see what is meant by a
"State of Life," and how one state of life is distinguished from another.

By "State of Life" I understand a certain fixed
or constant manner of living, which, by the sum
of duties it lays upon us, the difficulties it gives
rise to, or the helps it procures us in the spiritual
or moral order, is clearly marked off from every
other manner of living.

For the sake of greater clearness I will explain
this definition :—

A state of life is a position in the world, a
manner of being and acting, better than those of
people who have no fixed position, or who act as
if they had none. A state of life, therefore, supposes a certain perfection, and at the same time a
certain stability. A transitory position, determined
by momentary duties, does not constitute a true
"state of life;" and those who, in speaking of the

B

states of men, have discussed, for instance, the state
of pilgrims,* have attached themselves to the ety-
mological sense of the word " state " (status), and
have forgotten its real meaning.   Properly, we can
only call a " state of life " those conditions in which
we are fixed by permanent duties, and in which
we obtain help from Heaven by reason of these
duties, in order to accomplish the law of God and
answer the call of Providence.   Notice that we
shall here consider states of life only in their
source—which is the decrees of Providence,—and
in their end—which is the happiness of men in
this life and in the next.   Thus we may distinguish the different states that a Christian can
embrace by the duties, the difficulties and the
helps which these states suppose in the spiritual
and moral order.   We shall not consider at all the
purely temporal advantages, nor the consequences
to society, otherwise so worthy of attention, which
are their results.   We only look at states of life in
their relation to conscience and to salvation.

From this general point of view writers of considerable importance, ancient as well as modern,
have distinguished only *two* states of life among
Christians.

" In the Church of Christ," says Eusebius, " there
are two rules of life, or two manners of living.   The
first, which is spiritual and raised far above ordinary
life, eschews marriage, the care of perpetuating the
race, goods and riches ; it keeps aloof from ordinary

* 1: g. Father Busaeus : *Of the States of Men.*

and common life in order to cleave solely to the service and worship of God, through a powerful attraction of love for the things of heaven.

"Those who have embraced it, being dead to the life of men, holding to the earth only by their bodies, whilst raised up by their affections even into the heavens, like to God, despise mortal life; they are consecrated in the midst of the rest of men unto the God of the universe, not by sacrifices and blood-shedding, by libations or the sweet smell of victims, by smoke, fire, and the burning-up of bodies; but by the pure and seasonable faith of the worship of truth, by the affections of a heart unsoiled, by words and actions quickened by virtue. These offerings they present to the Deity, and thus exercise the priesthood for themselves and for those who share their faith. Such is the perfect life which Christianity has established.

"The other manner of living, less sublime and more adapted to human weaknesses, allows of marriage, free from sinful excesses, the care of perpetuating the race and the administration of goods. It points out the path of justice to those who are lawfully engaged in the warfare of the world; it teacheth those who apply themselves either to the tillage of the fields or to commerce, or to the other occupations of life, how they may acquit themselves religiously of these divers cares. For those who follow this manner of living there are marked out times for religious practices, days for instructions and for assisting at sermons.

"In this manner the New Alliance offereth to

these last a second degree suitable to the life they lead, in order that no one may be deprived of the benefits of the revelation of salvation, and that the whole human race, Greeks and barbarians, may enjoy the teaching of the Gospel."*

This beautiful definition of the two principal states of life which men embrace in the Church was quite sufficient for Eusebius of Cæsarea, who wrote for the pagans; and as it is true in its general idea it has found favour with some modern theologians.† But, looked at with reference to the end we propose to ourselves in treating of this matter, the definition appears to us insufficient.

In considering the *duties, difficulties* and *graces* inherent in the different manners of life which are followed in the Church and which enter into the scheme of Divine Providence, we are led to recognize *four* very distinct states of life: I mean the ecclesiastical state, or the priesthood; the religious state; the married state; and the state of voluntary celibacy in the world. These four states have each of them really duties of their own, particular dangers and special graces, as we are about to point out. We here speak of graver duties, which affect and modify the manner of living, and which have an influence upon conduct at large; spiritual dangers resulting from the position in which one is placed; and the graces attached by Providence to these states.

* Eusebius: *Evangelical Demonstrations*, book I., ch. viii., p 29 (ed. 1628).
† Suarez: *Of Religion*, vol. i.

I. For the ecclesiastical state, which Eusebius calls the first and the highest degree of moral life, the thing is easy to point out. The priest is chosen from among men in order to busy himself with the things of God on behalf of his brethren: it is for their welfare that he offers to Heaven sacrifices and prayers. He must, in virtue of his state, praise and glorify God by serving the altar. He gives himself to teaching, directing, sanctifying the people, and to becoming holy himself, because the God he serves is holiness by His essence.

Here, certainly, are special *duties* of wondrous sublimity!

This state, again, has *difficulties* which are altogether peculiar to itself. These difficulties are the result of the sublimeness of the functions, the weight of the duties and the extent of the obligations laid upon a man weak and frail, who cannot lift himself up to the height of this heavenly dignity, this God-like holiness, except by the aid of those graces and helps which God vouchsafes him and to which he ought to correspond continually and faithfully.

These *graces* are also quite peculiar to the priesthood. Firstly, it is by a Sacrament of Divine institution, by the Sacrament of Holy Order, that man is placed in this state. Next, the intimate relations which the priest constantly has with God—by the study of heavenly truths, by prayer, by the continual handling (if we may so speak) of things holy—surround a priest, in some sort, with an atmosphere of graces, whose Divine influence lifts

him above the common run of men, and places him
in certain respects in the ranks of the angels, the
constant ministers of the will of God.

II. The religious state, in its turn, brings with
it certain *duties*. The observance of the Evangelical counsels by vows of obedience, poverty and
perfect chastity, overrules all the thoughts, feeling
and acts of a true religious. The rule of the Order
which he has embraced traces out for him even his
least actions. He must aim at the highest degrees
of Christian perfection by the practices of the
monastic life ; he must hold in dread the maxims of
the world, and fly like a plague the pleasures and
ease of the age, in order to apply himself without
slacking to the exercises of prayer, humility, penance
and poverty. These duties do not exist to the same
degree and in the same manner in any other state ;
but in the religious state they overrule the whole of
life, even to its smallest details.

The *difficulties* proper to this state come from the
very perfection of the duties it imposes and the
natural unsteadiness of man. The loftier the end at
which we aim, the greater the striving necessary to
reach it, and the steadfastness required to keep up
that striving. There is no other state which so
effectually keeps at a distance the ordinary dangers
of spiritual life and the common causes of sin and
occasions of falling ; nor is there any other which
opens up more abundant springs of graces and
virtues : and in this respect the religious state bears
the palm from all the rest. But it is none the less
true that in this state there is needed a great faith-

fulness to grace, a deep contempt for the things of the world, a steadfast intention to serve God with generosity, and a complete renunciation of every other intention. These are, then, what, with reference to the weaknesses of the human heart, I call the special difficulties of the religious state.

As for the special *graces* which God attaches to it, they are manifest. I have just touched upon some of them ; and, in addition, I ask, Who fails to see the happiness of this life, so submissive, chaste and poor, altogether like that which our Divine Saviour led upon earth ? Who does not admire those fixed practices which overrule the whole man, which continually recall to him his duties, and by this very fact make easy to him their fulfilment ? Who can help taking note of this touching exclamation of our Saviour : Blessed are the poor in spirit, blessed are they who give themselves to chastity for the kingdom of heaven. If ye would be perfect, deny yourselves and follow Me ? There are blessings altogether peculiar attached to this beautiful and noble sacrifice of the vows, and it is to these blessings that we must attribute the holiness of that multitude of religious who have adorned the Church, and all the great works that the religious orders have done for the happiness and welfare of the Christian people.

III. The state of marriage also brings with it special *duties* for those who embrace it. Married people owe to each other a mutual affection, steadfast and pure, sincere respect and esteem, faithfulness under every trial, reciprocal patience, which

shall aid them in putting up with one another's
defects and forgiving each other's faults; the
Christian education of their children, however bad-
tempered, froward or headstrong they may be; the
superintendence of persons placed under them; the
care of their temporal concerns and the fortune of
their family: all these are duties peculiar to their
state—duties which the law of God imposes rigorously upon them—duties which cause, in truth,
certain difficulties of their own. The husband must
respect his wife and protect her weakness: the
wife must respect her husband and obey him, as
the head of the family, in all things not contrary
to the law of God. Both will have to answer
before God for the good or evil they have done to
the persons whose existence and management God
has entrusted to them.

This state, which appears so easy, has also its
difficulties, and these difficulties surpass the idea
that people commonly have of them. "She that
is married," saith St. Paul, "thinketh on the
things of the world, how she may please her husband," whilst "the unmarried woman thinketh on
the things of the Lord."* This state so absorbs
the thoughts and affections, that God's part seems
to dwindle in the hearts of those who have embraced it. Whilst the moral powers are weakened
under the empire of sense, the ordinary trials of
life seem doubled for persons engaged in marriage.
This is what St. Paul foretells them, when he

* 1 Cor. vii. 34.

declares that "such shall have tribulation of the
"flesh." * "Alas!" cries out St. Jerome, "it was
believed that if marriage brought with it cares and
troubles, it would at least ensure the pleasures of
the flesh: but there is no such thing. The
Apostle teaches that even in the flesh we must
look for tribulation." † Indeed, in the state of
marriage, how many troubles and vexations are
there not, for example, awaiting Christian parents
when their children fall into vice and forget their
duties! What tears at the death of a well-beloved
son or daughter! What bitterness, what despair
at the loss of a husband or a wife! In order to
increase the patrimony of the family, what temptations to give way to avarice, or to have recourse
to unjust ways! What disasters are not brought
down by wars, inclement seasons, unlucky undertakings, or the malice of others! Christian men
and women, who desire to keep themselves unshaken
in the midst of these vicissitudes and temptations,
must reckon on an assistance altogether special from
Heaven; for human strength is quite insufficient
to overcome such numerous and serious difficulties.

But these special *helps* are never wanting to
Christian spouses. The Sacrament of Matrimony
was instituted to sanctify their union, and to assure
them, not only the increase of sanctifying grace
that is given them when they receive it, but also
the heavenly helps which they need in all the events

* 1 Cor. vii. 28.
† *Against Jovinian* book I., § 13 (vol. ii., p. 259, edit.
Vallarsi).

of their life in order to accomplish the duties which the conjugal state imposes upon them. The many fathers and mothers of families who have reached a high degree of holiness bear witness that this state does not impede the way of salvation. More than this, St. Paul declares that a Christian mother is saved by bringing up her children well. This state may, therefore, become for faithful souls a fruitful source of merits and a means of salvation.

IV. Lastly, celibacy in the world, when it is voluntary and embraced out of choice, also constitutes a state of life. When it is sanctioned by simple vows or by a serious resolution, celibacy imposes, upon the men or women who profess it, the *duties* of shunning and flying from the pleasures of the world, which are generally the rocks virtue makes shipwreck upon ; and of faithfully and steadfastly making use of the means of sanctification necessary for preserving the heart pure and perfectly submissive to God.

The *dangers* of this state consist in the fact that we thereby contract part of the obligations of the cloister, without having around us that solitude, that silence, and those exercises of piety that form the bulwark, the support and the strength of the religious.

In this state the simple vows or the sacrifice of a good will, with the firm resolution of persevering in the ways of virtue, of conquering the world, the devil and the flesh, always bring down *graces* proportional to the greatness and holiness of the undertaking ; for our dear Lord never allows Himself to be overcome in generosity.

It is noteworthy that each of the four states of life of which the children of God can make choice obtains a special sanctification which becomes the principle of its stability: a remark that applies particularly to the three first. The priesthood and marriage are sanctified by a sacrament, and the religious state by vows; while celibacy in the world may be sanctified by simple vows, or by a sincere offering of self and a pious resolution. We see that Divine Providence has, in a manner, instituted and sanctified these four states, as four manners of life suited to the wants of the faithful, and well-calculated to make easy to God's children, in the midst of the miseries and distractions of this world, the great work of their salvation.

But ought we to reckon only *four* states of life? For there are some writers who count a greater number.

As for ourselves, however, besides the four states of life which we have just described, we know only *professions*, which have no sensible influence upon the manner of life, and have not as their foundation a special disposition of Providence. In the spiritual and moral order these professions count as things indifferent. Thus, from the time of embracing a secular life in the world, whether a man engage himself in the magistracy, take to the bar, enlist in the army, practice medicine, or devote himself to commerce, he will always find himself in one of the four *states of life* that we have pointed out, nor will he depart from it by embracing one or other of these *professions*. The duties which these professions impose—as that of justice in the judge, sincerity in the lawyer, bravery in the soldier, learning in the physician, uprightness in the tradesman—are general duties which everybody must fulfil to a certain extent, and which in these professions require only a more extensive, faithful and constant application. Providence leaves these professions open to our choice, as certain grades of society in which each one may fix himself, in order to find in it an occupation suited to his tastes and talents and to the well-being and rank of his family. They never become otherwise than indifferent, except in cases where they are rendered dangerous on account of certain personal propensities; if, for instance, a magistrate, yielding to avarice, were to barter justice; or if a soldier, overcome by idleness, were to give himself up to libertinism; or if a man of business, overruled by vain ambition, were to ruin his family; or if a doctor, through lack of skill, were to injure his patients. In this case a profession, indifferent in itself, would become truly hurtful, and would have to be abandoned by those who, by their weakness, have become unable to acquit themselves of it without offending God or compromising their salvation. But all this is purely accidental.

But would not widowhood, at least, form a fifth state of life?

We do not think that it strictly merits the name. Widowhood, as regards duties, difficulties and spiritual helps, shares with the two states, between which it occupies the middle place, without itself constituting a state properly so called. It is the consequence of the married state, a part of whose obligations it retains: for instance, that of bringing up children in a Christian manner, of caring for their fortune and of obtaining a settlement for them. It resembles the state of voluntary celibacy in the world by its obligation of employing the same means of sanctification and of flying the same dangers. Widowhood, at least in our days, has not a particular sanctification by the rites of the Church; still, it may adopt that of the perfect life in the world, with which it is identified the moment it is embraced by choice and from a religious motive.

However, there is nothing to prevent the treating of the duties of widows or widowers, explaining the advantages of widowhood and its merits according to faith—as has been done by St. Ambrose, St. Augustine, St. John Chrysostom, and other holy Doctors of the Church—in order to encourage in the practice of Christian virtues those persons who are in this state, and to preserve them more effectually from the ordinary dangers to salvation.

CHAPTER II.

Of the Nature of Vocation to a State of Life, and of the Obligations it imposes.

In ordinary and familiar language natural inclination, or even an unreflecting inclination for any occupation, is called *a vocation* or *calling*.

In the language of Holy Writ mention is made
of vocation to the faith,* vocation to grace,† and
vocation to a higher perfection.‡

It is not with vocations of this sort that we are
concerned in handling the all-important question of
a state of life.

The vocation of which we speak is a *disposition
of Divine Providence, preparing, inviting, and
sometimes even obliging a Christian soul to embrace
one state of life in preference to another—a disposition which is ordinarily manifested by the qualities,
feelings and position of the person called.*

It was by a vocation of this sort that the twelve
apostles of Our Lord were called to the apostleship,
and by such a vocation must all the ministers of
God be called to the priesthood, in order to enter it
worthily. St. Paul speaks of this vocation when he
says: "Neither doth any man take the honour of
the priesthood to himself, but he that is called by
God, as Aaron was."§   And in speaking of common
callings: "Let every man abide in the same calling
in which he was called."‖

Let us explain the definition we have just given
of a vocation.

A vocation is a "disposition of Divine Providence," which rules and directs everything mightily

---

* "Many are *called*" (Matt. xx. 16).
† "In one hope of your *calling*" (Eph. iv. 4; Gal. i.
16, etc.).
‡ "All men take not this word" (Matt. xix. 11, etc.).
§ Heb. v. 4.   ‖ 1 Cor. vii. 20.

and sweetly. It does not ordinarily consist in an immediate and sensible revelation, but in the succession of a host of circumstances which God conducts and combines in such a manner as to lead the faithful soul sweetly to its destined end. Thus, when God resolved to raise the boy Joseph above his brothers, He made the very jealousy of these unnatural brothers an instrument of His Providence, and employed it in order to carry the holy Patriarch to the height of power and greatness. When it pleaseth Him to guide a soul to a state of perfection, He directs its steps, watches over its affections, inflames and tempers them; He speaks to it with an inward voice that engages its attention, confirms its will, and thus prepares it from afar and by different trials for a definite resolution. Sometimes He dries up this soul with the winds of tribulation, sometimes He overwhelms it with a torrent of graces; He breathes into it a horror of vice and a love of virtue; by that Divine art which *He* alone possesses of bending and overruling hearts, He makes it detest that which before it loved, and love that which hitherto it had held in abhorrence. When, on the contrary, it pleaseth Him to turn away a soul from a state of perfection, He hides from it the charms of that state, or makes it fear the burden, and thus keeps it back in the ordinary paths of piety and virtue.

This unseen, though real, action of God upon souls can only be attributed to His Providence. " I know, O Lord," saith the Prophet Jeremiah, " that the way of a man is not his; neither is it

in a man to walk and to direct his steps."*   " But
I have put my trust in Thee, O Lord," cries out
David; " I said: Thou art my God; my lots are
in Thy hands."† And the Apostle St. Paul, explaining the intentions of God's goodness in the
distribution of states, writes to the Corinthians :
" Every one hath his proper gift from God; one
after this manner and another after that. . . .
As the Lord hath distributed to every one, as God
hath called every one, so let him walk."‡ He
could not have expressed to us in clearer terms
that God distributes states of life according to
His own will and pleasure, and that He grants
them according to each one's qualities as the most
precious gifts of His Divine bounty.

This disposition of Providence is full of sweetness. It prepares the subject for the duties of
the state which it destines for him, by forming in
him suitable qualities ; and invites him to it by
inspiring him with a taste for it. Sometimes it
acts powerfully and speedily ; at other times by
degrees and slowly. Hence, in the one case, sudden and unshaken resolutions ; in the other, resolutions arrived at with difficulty, and long deferred.
In every case God speaks to the soul, and increases
the power of His voice, until He has produced a
full and entire conviction in the mind and a deep
persuasion in the heart. We cannot, therefore,
give a truer name than that of *vocation* (or calling)

* Jer. x. 23.   † Ps. xxx. 15-16.   ‡ 1 Cor. vii. 17.

to an operation of Divine Providence which serves in some manner for speech and summons.

We must not lose sight of this principle that God's will manifests itself as regards vocations, sometimes by the inward dispositions which it creates in the soul, sometimes by outward events and sensible circumstances which make a choice easy. At times inward invitations urge us and lead us to a decision; at other times circumstances or events more clearly mark out the heavenly call and influence the will. This principle will be further on developed as is proper: here we shall go on with the commentary upon our definition, in order to describe in detail the different operations of grace in the souls that it calls to a special state.

We have said that Divine Providence *prepares*, *invites* and sometimes *obliges* the faithful to follow the call of Heaven. Thus it *prepares* by disposing the soul while yet at a distance; it invites by awaking its attention, calling forth its reflection and urging it to deliberation; lastly, the order or command of obedience which obliges it to follow the summons comes from certain inward or outward indications of the Divine will.

The question has often been discussed whether or not the sum of these indications, when they appear to lead to the choice of a perfect state, have always the authority of a law or rigorous precept. In other words, whether the vocation to a perfect state is always of strict obligation, or whether it is sometimes of simple counsel; whether it is always

c

allowable to the faithful thus called to prefer a
state less perfect to the perfect state which grace
calls them to.

In order to prove that vocation to a perfect state
never obliges strictly, the words of our Lord are
cited, when, speaking to His disciples, He said:
"If thou wilt be perfect, go, sell what thou hast
and give it to the poor, . . . and come, follow
me;"* and the words of the Apostle, who says:
"Now, concerning virgins, I have no commandment
of the Lord, but I give counsel. . . . I think,
therefore, . . . that it is good for a man so
to be."† Whence it is concluded that the perfect
life in the priesthood or in the religious state is
always of counsel and never of precept.

This reasoning is specious rather than sound.
To begin with, we must except from this doctrine extraordinary vocations, such as that of St.
Paul to the apostleship, which was manifested by
prodigies. Nextly, we must hold it as certain
that the obligation to follow a vocation is the more
rigorous in proportion as God's will has manifested
itself by more striking signs. Now this certainly
becomes, in some cases, of a very high degree, and
consequently may entail a strict obligation. For
my part, I make no doubt that, under many circumstances, the signs of a Divine vocation are, for
a Christian soul, equivalent to a rigorous precept.
The evidence of these signs at times leaves no doubt
whatsoever: after them it would be rash to believe

* Matt. xix. 21.   † 1 Cor. vii. 25-26.

that we may resist with impunity God's will, or reject without disobedience and without danger the graces which He offers and promises.

It happens, too, that there are certain souls of such disposition that they cannot save themselves in the world; whilst they can find in the priesthood or in the religious state sure and plentiful means of salvation. This is the opinion of St. Gregory the Great; a noteworthy opinion, of which we shall speak elsewhere.

Lastly, it may be that God has need of able and devoted pastors, men according to His own heart, for the service of His Church; wherefore He has the right to call them and to make use of them in accordance with His plans. To resist Him when one is called to a mission both sublime and necessary is to offend Him, to fail in an undoubted duty.

It is easy to bear out this reasoning by a comparison furnished us by the Gospel.

Good works, in general theory, are of counsel, and not of precept. Our Saviour recommends them to all the faithful in general; He does not enjoin any of them absolutely upon anybody. Nevertheless, certain works, which are of counsel for all, become of precept for those faithful who have need of them as an indispensable means of reconciling themselves with God and of living in virtue. Fasting and penance, for example, out of the times prescribed by the Church, are of counsel; and yet there are sinners who will never reach salvation without employing them. For such

these works of counsel become obligatory. It is
the same with vocation to the perfect life, whenever God's glory, the sanctification of souls, the
welfare of the Church, or the individual salvation
of the soul thus called is involved; and this we
must always suppose to be the case when God
speaks and invites in a pressing manner.

Finally, I will add that God rejects absolutely
from the priesthood Christians who are either incapable or unworthy of this sublime ministry; this is
a certainty, and, if proof were needed, the canons of
the Church would attest it. How, then, can we
believe that God does not call in the same absolute
manner, though by ordinary means, the souls which
He has selected for this state? Would He do
more, in the order of His providence, to keep away
the incapable and the unworthy from His sanctuary, than to enrol and consecrate to His service
the souls whom He destines to hold His place on
earth? Who can ever believe that the empire of
God, which overruleth all vocations, is less absolute over perfect vocations than over common ones?
Now God imposes upon many the common vocation; therefore He also imposes perfect vocations.
This reasoning leaves room for no reply.

We must, then, examine the signs of Divine
vocation, and, after having thoroughly sifted them
with the aid of a prudent director, we must generously resolve to embrace the state which the voice
of Heaven marks out for us. This is the only way
of finding peace, repose and happiness on earth, and
of securing our welfare for eternity.

CHAPTER III.

Of the Necessity of a Christian Deliberation in order to the Choice of a State of Life.

THE necessity for deliberation on the choice of a state of life is not general : there are many classes of the faithful, for whom the oracle of the Divine will is so clear, that they have neither inquiry nor effort to make in order to understand it.

Those, for instance, whom God calls, like Moses, Samuel or St. Paul, by making His presence sensible to them, or by speaking to them in human speech, can neither hesitate nor doubt ; they must cry out with the prophet, when they hear the voice of God : "Speak, Lord, for Thy servant heareth," * or else with the Apostle of the Gentiles : "Lord, what wilt Thou have me to do?"† These, however, are rare cases.

Those again whom birth or family duties fix without any doubt in the state of their parents have no examination to make. A prince who is the heir apparent of a kingdom, a princess whose alliance is destined some day to assure the public peace ; the only son of a widow, the daughter of a widower, who have to sustain their parents, and all Christians in analogous positions, must only think of fulfilling the duties common to the faithful, and those of the state in which they are fixed by force

---

* 1 Kings, iii. 10. † Acts ix. 6.

of circumstances. The Church knows so well the
ties of gratitude which bind children to their
parents, that, in certain cases, she permits a son
or daughter to leave the cloister and re-enter the
world, in order to assist and console the authors of
their life.

Cases of sickness, grave infirmities, incapacity, or
extreme youth render a deliberation useless. When
a person cannot fulfil the functions or accomplish
the duties of a certain state he is certainly not
called thereto. All investigation would be, in these
circumstances, superfluous : for a man is then called
to the common life and to the general duties of the
Christian people.

It also happens, sometimes, that young people, on
growing out of childhood, conceive an inclination
for embracing the clerical or the religious state. In
order to attain this object they engage in study,
applying themselves to the exercise of virtue, give
themselves to practices of piety, and under the
influence of Divine grace, and with the guidance
of able masters, they strengthen themselves day
by day in their pious resolution, without meeting
any obstacles to their project, without expe-
riencing doubts about the solidity of their vocation. These young people, strictly speaking, have
no need of a special deliberation : their behaviour
at college and under the paternal roof, the advice
they ask of their confessor, the straightforward
intention which enlivens them, the courage and
zeal with which they engage in the career of the
priesthood or of the religious life—all suffice to

give them full confidence in the choice which they
have made, and to dispense them from all further
deliberation.

A formal deliberation becomes absolutely necessary only in cases where there is a doubt about the
vocation: but in such cases it cannot be omitted.
It would be the very height of rashness to engage
onself in a state, the burden of which we were not
sure of being able to uphold, and in which we were
not certain of deserving Heaven's blessing. A step
of this importance ought not to be taken without
full knowledge for the purpose of, and of a nature
suited to, preventing useless and too-late regrets.
Every time there is doubt we must deliberate.

Doubt takes possession of the minds of youth,
especially in three cases, which I will describe.

I. There are certain characters naturally prone
to perplexity, timid and irresolute, which instinc-
tively recoil before every final resolution. As soon
as they put themselves face to face with the future,
their looks become troubled, their heart flutters ;
they advance, they step back again ; they turn to
right and to left without the power of fixing either
their ideas or their will. On the one hand they
feel themselves carried on towards God and the
ecclesiastical life; but, on the other hand, they
dread its burdens and obligations. They feel the
attractions of common life; but they feel convinced
that they will not save themselves in the world.
All their paths seem to abut on precipices.

The only manner of enlightening and deter-
mining such souls is to propose to them a regular

deliberation, in which they are to examine calmly
and dispassionately how much solid foundation and
how much exaggeration there is both in their desires and in their fears.   If they give themselves to
this exercise they will very soon be enlightened,
and they will confidently make a resolution of
which they will never afterwards repent.

II.   There are other youths who, having received
a careful education, and one sometimes superior to
their condition, feel themselves moved to embrace
the ecclesiastical state as that career whose approaches present the fewest obstacles.   Their social
position not being very brilliant, they hope to elevate both themselves and their families by embracing a state which enjoys universal esteem.   A
father, a mother, or a benefactor look upon the
entry of their son, or *protégé*, as the case may be,
into the ecclesiastical state as a thing finally decided.
But the young man, when he weighs in the balance
of the sanctuary the motives which induce him to
embrace this state, trembles and shudders.   He
fears lest purely temporal considerations be his first
motive; he doubts whether his virtue has been
tried sufficiently to bear the burden of the priesthood.   He is not quickened with these sentiments
of lively piety and ardent faith which he notices in
those of his fellow-students who are preparing for
the ecclesiastical career.   He asks himself how he
—weak as he is, with passions but half extinguished,
with evil habits perhaps scarcely kept under—will
be able to acquit himself of the duties of this state ?
how he will be able to appear in the temple of the

Lord, and to persevere in the practice of priestly virtues? He would like to follow the external impulse exerted on him; but he feels an inward force holding him back.

Such a youth would be very guilty were he to embrace the ecclesiastical state before examining seriously and before God whether he be called thereto.

III. It also happens that young men, favoured by the gifts of nature and of fortune, hear from their infancy in the bottom of their heart that Divine voice that was heard by the son of Anna, the wife of Phanuel: "Samuel, Samuel!" But they hesitate to answer: "Speak, Lord, for thy servant heareth." The hopes of a great fortune, the prospect of a brilliant position, an all-smiling future, family usages, the expectations of parents, and, we may say, a natural attraction to sensible and worldly things, make them neglect this inward voice of grace and cause it to seem troublesome. They would wish not to hear it; sometimes, even, they would wish to silence it. But when they reflect before God upon the future that stands before them, when they invoke the aid of our Blessed Lady, their angel-guardian and their patron saints, in order to know what they have to do to work out their salvation in this world; when they say to our Saviour, as did the young man in the Gospel: " What good shall I do that I may have life everlasting ?" *—the voice of God redoubles its loudness and says more strongly than ever, "Samuel, Samuel! "

* Matt. xix. 16.

The only means of dissipating the doubts which
arise from these two tendencies, and of putting an
end to the inward conflict which they stir up, is to
apply oneself to a prudent deliberation, in order to
distinguish the voice of God calling to a perfect
state, from disquieting whims and from simple
illusions which trouble the soul and merit our contempt. To decide without examination in such a
case is to expose oneself to many miseries, vexations
and regrets ; in some cases to peril one's salvation.

Deliberation, which is *necessary* in doubt, is
always *useful* to Christian youth ;. at least in order
to a better understanding of the obligations and
duties of the state they embrace, and, according to
the expression of Holy Writ, in order to know one's
ways. "They that fear the Lord," saith the Holy
Spirit," will seek after the things that are well-
pleasing to Him."* "My son," saith the Holy
Spirit again, "do thou nothing without counsel,
and thou shalt not repent when thou hast done."†
Every Christian youth, when about to choose his
career in life, ought, therefore, to cry out with
David : "Make the way known to me wherein I
should walk." ‡ For affairs less important than the
choice of a state of life we ask advice, deliberate,
and decide not without a full knowledge of the
case. How much more ought we not, according to
the expression of Holy Writ, to consult the mouth
of the Lord, and to place our person under His

* Ecclus. ii. 19.   † *Ib.* xxxii. 24.
‡ Ps. clxii. 8.

special protection before embracing a state of life?
Those who decide blindly in so important an affair
are almost like the man in the Gospel who began
to build a tower and could never finish it: "This
man began to build, and was not able to finish," *
because he had not reflected beforehand on the difficulties of his undertaking.

We must, then, keep to these two general rules:
first, that a prudent deliberation is always *useful*,
save in a few very rare cases; second, that it is
absolutely *necessary* every time that it is doubtful
what God's will may be in this important matter.

CHAPTER IV.

Of the Conditions of a Good Deliberation.

THE Gospel tells us that the householder sendeth
labourers into his vineyard at all hours of the day;
that he calls some at the third hour, others at the
sixth, others at' the eleventh; in order to teach us
that God calls His children to the ecclesiastical or to
the perfect life, some from their infancy, others in
the fulness of their age, others at the decline of
their days.

Whatever be the epoch of life at which the voice
of God appears to be heard, if this voice is not
clear and distinct, it is necessary to deliberate

* Luke xiv. 30.

seriously in order to recognize it and to catch its meaning with certainty.

In youth, the time most suitable for applying oneself to this examination is, almost always, between the ages of 16 and 20.   ·

The success of the deliberation depends in great measure upon the manner in which it is made. We will here state, in a few words, what are the conditions on which we may hope to succeed in it.. We will show that it is first of all necessary to procure a good director, and to retire for some days into a pious solitude. As interior dispositions, we must bring the spirit of prayer, a great purity of heart and a humble submission to the Divine will. Lastly, it is necessary to proceed all through this business with much order and method.

We will develope these points in succession :—

§ I. Of the exterior conditions for a good deliberation.

If God were Himself to explain His will to men they would have hardly any need of advice. But it is very rarely that He speaks personally to mortals. to explain to them in detail the law of their duties, He is wont to guide His children by the ministry of certain men, whom He fills with His spirit, clothes with His authority, and constitutes the chiefs of His people. Thus He raised up Moses to deliver Israel from the bondage of Egypt; Josue to lead the Hebrews into the Promised Land: thus also He chose His twelve apostles, and founded the Catholic Church upon a sacred hier-

archy, whose members are the fathers, counsellors
and guides of the faithful.

In directing St. Paul to Ananias our heavenly
Master has pointed out to us what we must do
when we have need of direction and advice. He
would have us choose from among the ministers
of the Church an arbiter of our conscience, who
should be to us a guide and a support. The help
of a prudent director is never more needful for us
than at the moment when, uncertain, disquieted
and troubled, we are preparing to ask the Lord
and to discriminate the sound and meaning of
His voice amid the din that is made in and
about us.

. He would be very rash who should hope to tra-
verse by himself with success the difficult parts
of such an examination. To him undoubtedly
could we apply those words of the Holy Spirit:
"Woe to him that is alone, for when he falleth
he hath none to lift him up."*

The need of a good director evidently results
from the difficulty of the undertaking. It is
required to appreciate the advantages and difficulties of one or several states of life, of which
we have no experience; to search into our fitness
and personal dispositions; to discriminate amid a
crowd of emotions of the soul those which come
from God and those which come from the flesh.
This is a very complicated and difficult business,
which a young man cannot settle without the help

* Eccles. iv. 10.

of another. Hence, a good director is indispensable to him.

When he has found him he will abandon himself to the guidance of the man of God with unbounded confidence; he will explain to him his views and his ideas, open to him his heart, communicate to him his projects and desires, discover to him even his weaknesses and mortal wounds, acknowledge to him his evil inclinations, his faults and his falls, make known to him his fears and hopes for the future; show him, in a word, the depths of his soul, in order that this counsellor may act towards him as a father, a physician and a friend. He must be careful, too, not to conceal from him the graces and favours that God has already bestowed upon him. If, for instance, he has had from childhood a decided taste for piety and the things of God; if the frequentation of the Holy Sacraments is for him full of delights; if he feels a great attraction to prayer, a great zeal for the salvation of souls and the glory of God; if he feels in his heart disgust and fear of the world, a horror of sin, a lively love for the practice of virtues such as purity, mortification, humility, obedience; he may not conceal these workings of grace from his director, but he must expose them to him with candour and simplicity, as if addressing Jesus Christ Himself. Let him, therefore, enter into all the details capable of enlightening his director and guiding his judgment; telling him about what age he has seriously thought either of settling in the world or of embracing the perfect life; under what circumstances these desires or whims oftenest return; whether on feast-days, at the time of Communion, or in the midst of games and dissipation; whether he be followed and besieged by these thoughts, whether he have repeatedly repulsed them; whether they rejoice or sadden his heart. All these questions, and others, too, which a prudent director will put to him, must receive a full solution.

The fulfilling of this duty will throw a great light on the whole deliberation, and will diffuse calm and peace in the soul of him who is deliberating. "The good counsels of a friend," saith the Holy Ghost, "are sweet to the soul."* This word will be accomplished literally in all those who consult the Lord with faith and simplicity by asking of His ministers.

In the second place, we must be convinced that such a deliberation cannot be made in the midst of our ordinary occupations or of the distractions of the world. The Holy Spirit, speaking of a soul whom He would illumine with His heavenly light, saith: "I will lead her into the wilderness, and I will speak to her heart."† If we wish to hear the voice of Heaven we must seek a quiet and solitary place, where we may be face to face with God; we must quit for some days the shifting scene of the world, in which, perhaps, we have found the principal source of our doubts and inquietudes. We must imitate the Baptist, who buried himself in the

---

* Prov. xxvii. 9.　　† Osee ii. 14; cf. Is. ii. 3.

desert in order to prepare himself for his sublime
career, and our Divine Master Himself, who passed
forty days in the wilderness before beginning His
preaching., We must follow the example of the
holy anchorites, who sought God in the remotest
parts of the desert and lived in silence so deep that
they feared lest even their own voice should disturb
the peace or spoil the charms of their pious solitude.   Whether we find shelter beneath the shades
of a cloister, or whether we retire to a friend's
house, we must be solicitous to break with our
ordinary occupations in order to busy ourselves
entirely, for some days, in a holy retreat, with the
all-important resolution which is to fix the duties
of our after-life.

So much for exterior dispositions.

§ II. Of the interior conditions for a good deliberation.

. As I have already indicated, in order to succeed
in this deliberation, we must bring to it the spirit of
prayer, a great purity of conscience, and a perfect
conformity to the will of God.

This deliberation has for its end to put us in
communication with God in order to know His
will: prayer, therefore, must begin this spiritual
transaction.   First of all, ask the light of the Holy
Ghost in order to consider all the things of this
world from the standpoint of eternity; next, ask
courage to despise the world and the flesh, in order
to judge everything according to the spirit and

faith; lastly, ask the grace of a good and salutary deliberation.

Beyond this, we must address ourselves to our Lord Jesus Christ, our dear Saviour, through the intercession of the Blessed Virgin Mary, of our angel guardian, and of our patron saints, in order to obtain strength to embrace courageously the state which Divine Providence destines for us, and to persevere in it, with His grace, to our last breath. In our griefs, our anguish and our anxiety, it is only at the feet of the crucifix that we must seek the vivid lights, the sweet tears, the pure consolations, which were the share of Mary Magdalen at the foot of the cross.

Sin is like a crushing weight, which prevents the soul from rising up to God and communing with Him. It darkens the intellect, weighs down the will, keeps down the soul and pins it to the earth. The disorderly love of creatures stifles in the soul the love of God, and extinguishes all strength and all energy for good. If we have had the misfortune to lose grace, submit to the yoke of the passions, and give ourselves to vice, in order to deliberate successfully, we must, first of all, break with the devil, shake off the yoke of sin, return to an innocent life, and purify our heart from all manner of stain and wilful offence against God. For this end a general confession will be very useful. It will serve, not only to reconcile the sinful soul to God, but it will also procure the penitent a deeper knowledge of himself, it will excite in him a more generous contrition, and will enable him, by the

D

remembrance of his past faults, to foresee and forestall better the dangers of the future.

Young people who have had the happiness of
preserving their baptismal innocence may have
recourse to a general confession in order to make
themselves more pleasing to God, by deploring
before Him their venial faults, their infidelities to
grace, their negligences and their forgetfulnesses.
Whilst recalling in spirit all that God has hitherto
done for their sanctification and the little they
have themselves done for His glory, they will feel
themselves penetrated with the desire of fulfilling
henceforward His holy will in all things, and of
forearming themselves against the dangers of luke-
warmness and laxity. The purer and holier the
heart is, the more pleasing is it to God; the more
does it merit those Divine lights which mark out to
us the way to heaven. To succeed in this pious
deliberation, we also need a perfect indifference of
will, and a humble submission to the decrees of
Divine Providence, whatsoever they may be.

Indeed, wherefore is such a deliberation under-
taken, except to know God's will? Among two
or three possible conditions, we wish to know that
one which God imposes upon us or expects from
us. If our mind is made up beforehand, we have a
sensible leaning for one choice to the detriment of
the rest; there is no more examination, discussion
or inquiry, but a resolution already taken—a deliberation in this case is aimless.

In order to keep in a perfect equilibrium of will,
we must, above all, take precautions against any

influence that may be exercised by a blind or too
keen attachment to the goods of earth, the con-
veniences of life, the attractions and ties of family.
Les us put aside, for a few hours, birth, fortune,
kinsfolk, friends, talents, successes; I will even say
passions, vices, weaknesses, infirmities, inclinations,
faults; not because we must consider all these
things as henceforward irrelevant (for the time will
come when we must occupy ourselves seriously with
their consideration), but because we must not
allow ourselves to be overruled by these affections
or memories, but must let them enter into our
deliberation, each in its turn, one after the other,
in a becoming manner, looking at them from the
standpoint of faith and of the examination in which
we are engaged.

It is not necessary to distress ourselves in order
to require a perfect indifference with regard to each
of these objects in particular; it is enough to put
aside the affections or apprehensions which break
the balance of the will and prevent our feeling ourselves, from the very beginning of the deliberation,
superior to fear and to hope.

A marked preference for the ecclesiastical or
religious life, if it disturbs or preoccupies us, is
also quite as contrary to the indifference which we
here exact, as a violent inclination for common life
in the world. On whatever side the affections weigh
us down, they disturb the equilibrium of the will,
and prevent that perfect submission to God's will,
which is the starting-point of every Christian
deliberation.

In order to deliberate well, therefore, let us apply ourselves to this perfect indifference, which makes us accept beforehand the decrees of Heaven, whatever they may be.

§ III. Of the order to be followed in this deliberation.

We may divide the time of the deliberation into three nearly equal parts. The first will be devoted to meditating on the fundamental truths of salvation; the second to examining the nature of different states of life and the signs of each vocation; the third is applying these truths to one's own case and making a final resolution.

If we dedicate five or six days to making a retreat and discussing before God the business of our vocation, we should give the two first to meditating upon the great truths of salvation. It is especially in its relation to salvation that the choice of a state of life is of such immense importance; we must, therefore, make this choice with our eyes directed towards God, our mind occupied with heaven and eternity, our soul all filled with thoughts of the four last things.

Here, for instance, is a series of truths which we must go through and penetrate ourselves with :

God has created me for His glory and my own happiness. If I cling to Him I shall be happy; if I offend Him I am working out my own misery.

God has sovereign right over me : this right He will exercise in time and eternity, in the name of either His mercy or His justice.

All creatures are good or evil for me, according to the manner in which I use them, according as they bring me near to or remove me away from the God who has created me.

Life is short ; life passes like a shadow : it is in the hands of the Lord.

At every instant death is coming nearer to me : I know not the hour when it will meet me.

I shall be judged for eternity according to the merits I have acquired in this fragile and fugitive life.

In fine, salvation gained, all is gained; salvation lost, all is lost. No middle term for me : either the glory of the saints in the highest of the heavens, or the torments of the damned in the depths of hell. And that *for eternity !*

Since this is the case, I submit myself lovingly to the sovereign will of God. I wish to make use of the goods of earth in such manner that I may not lose the happiness of heaven. I will do all to gain the deathless crown, whatever it may cost me. I will, therefore, be God's in life and in death.

When we are thoroughly penetrated with these cardinal truths, we must review in spirit the ideas that have already been set forth regarding states of life. In the following chapters we shall learn the signs of a Divine vocation and the signs of non-vocation. For instance, I will suppose a young man who believes himself called to the ecclesiastical state, and who feels nevertheless a certain repugnance or a certain dread in accepting the obligations that this holy state imposes. I would not have him

apply to himself the ideas we have suggested, before
he shall have arrived at a state of perfect indifference by meditating on the truths of salvation, and
formed a just and full idea of what is called *vocation*
in general, and of what constitutes vocation to the
ecclesiastical state in particular, as well as of the
signs which indicate Divine vocations. Until he
has grasped this short and easy theory he should
not busy himself with his own person. Only after
having meditated upon and comprehended this
theory will he be able usefully to apply it to himself, considering, on the one hand, the state of his
mind and heart; and, on the other, the signs of
the Divine will. In the rules which we have
sketched he will find a sort of mirror in which he
may behold himself; a standard of comparison with
which to measure his sentiments, dispositions and
ideas. He will there see that innocency of life,
zeal, inward inspirations, ardent desires, are certain
signs of vocation to the ecclesiastical state. The
intimate knowledge that he has acquired of the state
of his soul will permit him to see whether he can
find in himself these signs or not; and he will thus
arrive, without effort, at a conclusion which will end
the deliberation and fix his resolution.

I say, *without effort.* It is none the less possible
that, at the moment of decision, nature may give
him up to a last assault, in order to stifle the voice
of grace, and may raise a furious storm in the depths
of his heart. This breaking out again of struggle
and contest must not dismay him : it is the agony
of corrupt or too natural instincts. Let him, then,

have recourse to the guide of his conscience, let him raise his mind and heart to Heaven, let him invoke Mary, his good angel, his patron saints, and he will win a complete victory after this last combat.

It is in the midst of perfect quiet, in the centre of this bright light, when the mind clearly perceives the expression of the Divine will, that the youth engaged in this deliberation will decide for the state which Heaven marks out for him. Whether God call him to common life in the world, or whether He call him to perfect life in the priesthood or the cloister, he will accept the sentence which Providence pronounces over him, and offering himself to God for evermore, with generosity and gratitude, he will now only think of the means of executing without delay his definitive resolution.

This calm and well-weighed resolution will not only put an end to the doubts which afflicted him before his deliberation, but will also remove the perplexities and doubts which may arise in the future. The attacks of human inconstancy, unfortunately only too common, which at certain epochs of life are undergone by the most generous souls, and which tend to disgust them with the state they have chosen, will never shake his courage or poison his existence. When clouds gather around him and darken his mind, he will recover himself by the thoughts and memories of those hours of unsullied brightness during which he fixed his choice. He will say to himself, "If I now feel vexation, weariness or regret, it is because I have forgotten God and neglected my duties. I no longer see things in

the light which enlightened me during my deliberation.   This is the cause of my trouble and my error.
I *could* not be mistaken then : I am mistaken now."
This reasoning, and a sincere turning to God, will
suffice to dissipate all clouds and to re-establish
perfect peace.

But, you will say, if everybody gave themselves
to such a deliberation, everybody would embrace
the ecclesiastical or the religious state: the laical
state would be abandoned.

This is a mistake, resulting from a great mis-
understanding.   To avoid this mistake, it is enough
to know that a Christian deliberation, such as we
have just described, does not *give* a vocation, but
manifests it, if it exists.   God alone is the Author
of all vocations ; and, as in the counsels of His
Divine wisdom He calls not all the faithful to
the ecclesiastical or religious state, it is impossible
that a Christian deliberation should determine all
to embrace this state.   God destines the greater
number of the faithful to common life in the world,
and He dispenses vocations to the common life with
as much sovereignty as vocations to the perfect life.
We as grievously disobey Him if we engage in the
ecclesiastical state against His will, as if we shun
this state when He calls to it.   The Church, His
interpreter, even utters more anathemas against the
rash ones who invade His sanctuary without vocation than against the feeble-hearted who hear the
voice of the Lord and obey it not.

If all the faithful, before embracing a state of
life, were to consult the will of God and conform

to its decrees, piety, brotherly charity, love of duty
and peace would return everywhere, and we should
see perfect order and a happiness hitherto unknown
on earth reign all over the world.

CHAPTER V.

Of the Ecclesiastical State, and of Vocation thereto.

ALTHOUGH all the faithful, and especially those
whom God calls, or seems to call, to the service of
the altar, have the highest idea of the dignity and
holiness of the ecclesiastical state, it is fitting here
to expose, to those youths who are deliberating on
the choice of a state of life, the origin, sublimity
and advantages of the priesthood.

In this chapter we are going to show them that
God is the Author of vocations to the ecclesiastical
state, in an altogether special manner, by a sort of
extraordinary influence which is not observable in
other vocations. We will also prove that vocation
to the ecclesiastical state is, for him who obtains
it, both a great honour and a great happiness.

In the following chapters we will indicate the
signs by which to recognize vocation to the ecclesiastical state, and those by which to recognize
non-vocation thereunto.

In order to render complete the elements of the
pious deliberation, which we have described in the
preceding chapter, we will develope the motives
which oblige the young man called by God to the

priesthood to follow the invitation of Heaven, and
him who is not called to respect the prohibition.

By the aid of these reflections we may pronounce
sentence with full knowledge of the case.

§ I. Vocation to the ecclesiastical state comes
from God in a special manner.

God, who governs the moral, as well as the
physical, order, disposes all vocations at His good
pleasure; but He reserves to Himself a special
sovereignty and right over ecclesiastical vocations.
Not content with instituting the priesthood as a
sacred dignity, as a consecrated ministry on whose
exercise true religion depends, He has willed at
all times Himself to mark out those who may be
lawfully clad with this ministry and those who are
to be set aside. Under the law of nature and under
the written law, as well as under the law of the
Gospel, God chooses his ministers and consecrates
them to His glory and to the welfare of His people.

Let us cast a brief glance over the three epochs
that we have indicated; let us examine the conditions of the priesthood, first of all in the epoch
which extended from the first revelation made to
Adam until the day when God dictated His Ten
Commandments to Moses on Mount Sinai; next
let us see how the priesthood was constituted after
the promulgation of the written law until the
promulgation of the Gospel; let us then recall the
nature of the new priesthood which our Saviour
inaugurated during the Last Supper, and which will
henceforth subsist to the end of time.

I. Under the law of nature it was the first-born
of each family who were vested with the priesthood
and who exercised it by offering sacrifices to God
and by making public prayer in the midst of, and
in the name of, the assembled people. There remain
several striking monuments of this remarkable
institution. According to Josephus, the Patriarch
Isaac sent his eldest son, Esau, to hunt, in order
that he might, by this .act of filial love, merit the
paternal benediction which was to transmit the
priesthood to him. Isaac gives this motive for it,
that, on account of his age, it is henceforth
impossible for him to fulfil the Divine service
which he owes to God.* It is, we may believe,
because he had sold his rights of primogeniture,
which embraced the priestly authority, that Esau
is called by St. Paul *a profane person*,† unworthy
of the priesthood, St. Isidore of Seville‡ following
it. Eucherius§ thinks that the fragrant vestment
which Jacob put on in order to secure by surprise
the blessing destined for Esau was the priestly
vestment of the family. The learned Tostatus‖
observes that, according to the ancients, Ruben,
the eldest son of Jacob, lost the priesthood on
account of the injury he had done his father; and

---

* Josephus: *Jewish Antiquities*, bk. i., c. 18.
† Heb. xii. 16.
‡ St. Isidore: *Commentary on Gen.* xxv.
§ *Commentary on Gen.* (attributed to St. Eucherius),
bk. ii., c. 45.
‖ Tostatus: *Commentary on Lev.* xxi. ques. 19 ; and on 1
Par. v. *Cf.* Gen. xxvii. 15, and Commentary.

that Judas, the fourth son of Jacob, inherited it
by the will of the holy Patriarch.

Moses, on descending from Sinai, caused an altar
to be prepared at the foot of the mountain, and
sacrifice to be there offered to the Lord by the
eldest born sons, as is indicated by the Chaldean
paraphrase of the text.* When this great prophet
had conferred the priesthood on all the children
of Aaron, according to God's command, Jethro,
priest of the Madianites, reproached him with not
having reserved this dignity for the first-born, at
least, according to ancient tradition.† The Jewish
doctors are agreed on this point, that before the
building of the Tabernacle the use of altars was
allowed, and the eldest son of each family sacri-
ficed thereon.‡ St. Paul has recourse to this institution to explain how our Lord Jesus Christ is the
Chief of the Church and the High Priest of the
faithful people, although not born of the tribe of
Levi, but from that of Juda.§ The mediator (he
says) is High Priest, as the "first born of every
creature," in virtue of the sacerdotal institution,
which existed before the written law, an institution
which the Apostle calls "according to the order of
Melchisidec,"‖ that is to say, according to the
order of that High Priest, who was priest of the
Most High under the empire of the law of nature.

* Exod. xxiv. 4, 5.
† Josephus: *Ant.* bk. iv.
‡ "Before the Tabernacle was built the use of altars was
allowed, and the eldest-born exercised their sacred func-
tions at it" (*Talmud*, Code of Sacrifice. xiv. § 4).
§ Colos. i. 15, 18.   ‖ Heb. vi. 20.

God, therefore, determined the sacerdotal state in the first age of the world, and only admitted those whom He had Himself chosen.

II. At the promulgation of the Law of Moses, the action of God on the institution and succession of the priesthood was still more striking.

He Himself chose the tribe of Levi to exercise the priesthood, although Levi had been the third son of Jacob. In this tribe He designated the family which should be honoured with the High Priesthood; and, in this family, the person who was to be first invested with it. The succession of the priesthood in its different grades was attached to the natural succession of the families, who were to remain for ever depositories of the sacred authority and were consecrated to the service of the Lord. The age and qualities requisite for the High Priest and other priests, the defects from which they were to be exempt, the rites of their consecration, the form of the sacrifices they had to offer—all were determined by God Himself with the utmost precision, in order that all might be of Divine authority in this state and ministry.

This priesthood lasted till the coming of our Saviour. When Caiphas rent his priestly garments before Jesus he signified, according to the ancient doctors, that the Mosaic priesthood had been abrogated and that a new one was established.

III. The institution of the priesthood by our Saviour stands forth clearly in every page of the Gospel. The solemn vocation of the Apostles is one of the most striking facts of the evangelic

history.   St. Mark tells how Jesus, having ascended
a mountain, "called unto Him whom He would
Himself," * and that He appointed twelve to remain
with Him and preach the Gospel.   And St. Luke
adds that He called them His "Apostles." †   As
He walked by the sea-side He saw Simon and
Andrew, his brother, casting their nets, and He
said to them : " Come ye after me, and I will make
you to be fishers of men.   And going on from
thence He saw other two brethren, James, the son
of Zebedee, and John, his brother, in a ship with
Zebedee, their father, mending their nets : and He
called them.   And they forthwith left their nets
and father and followed Him."‡   Later on our
Lord "saw a man sitting in the custom-house,
named Matthew, and He saith to him : Follow me.
And he arose up and followed Him."§

As He called to the apostleship those who had
not sought it, so He refused to admit those who
asked it.|| Thus He chose some and rejected others,
at the good pleasure of His wisdom and mercy.   In
order that there might be no doubt in this respect,
He said in express terms to His Apostles : "You
have not chosen me, but I have chosen you, and
have appointed you, that you should go and bring
forth fruit, and your fruit should remain."¶   "As
the Father hath sent me, I also send you." **
"Going, therefore, teach ye all nations.   .   .   .
teaching them to observe all things whatsoever I

---

* Mark iii. 13.   † Luke vi. 13.

‡ Matt. iv. 18—22.   § Matt. ix. 9. || Luke ix. 57—62.

¶ John xv. 16.   ** John xx. 21.

have commanded you."* Ye have just seen the
sacrifice of the New Law offered by me: "Do
this" yourselves "for a commemoration of me." †
"Whose sins you shall forgive, they are forgiven
them: and whose sins you shall retain, they are
retained." ‡ "Feed my lambs . . . Feed my
sheep." § "Behold, I am with you all days, even
to the consummation of the world."|| Vocation to
the apostleship, commission to teach the faith,
authority to impose the observance of the Commandments of God, power to offer the Sacrifice of
the New Covenant, pastoral care over the children of
God, perpetual co-operation on the part of God—in
a word, all that constitutes the priesthood has been
instituted in detail by Jesus Christ Himself.

And, in order that nobody may ignore His rights,
our Saviour utters terrible anathemas against those
who dare to usurp the sacred ministry. He calls
them thieves and robbers, who enter the sheepfold
by the window and not by the door, which is our
Lord Himself; He compares them to hirelings
who abandon the flock to the murderous fangs of
the wolves, instead of defending them.¶ He threa-
tens them with His wrath at the great day of
doom, when He will say to them, on their reminding
Him that they have prophesied in His name: "I
never knew you: depart from me." **

The sovereign dominion over the choice of ministers which God has reserved to Himself is written
on every page of the New Testament. Thus, we

---

* Matt. xxviii. 19, 20.   † Luke xxii. 19.
‡ John xx. 23.   § John xxi. 15—17. || Matt. xxviii. 20
¶ John x. 1—13.   ** Matt. vii. 23.

see that the Apostles committed to God the choice
of Judas' successor, as if the first of ecclesiastical
elections, the model of all others, could not be made
but by our Lord Jesus Christ Himself.* Before
laying hands upon St. Paul and Barnabas, the
Apostles waited for an oracle from heaven.†

The election of the first seven deacons was only
made after a fervent invocation of the Holy Ghost,
whose lawful interpreters the Apostles were. ‡

In the writings of St. Paul how often is homage
paid to this sovereign action of God over the choice
of His ministers ! The Apostle continually recalls
the fact that he has received the apostleship direct
from God, that God has called Him to this holy
state, that he is an apostle by a special grace of
God.§ He also lays down this rule that nobody can
intrude himself into the functions of the priesthood
on his own private authority, but that he must, like
Aaron, be called of God, by a special calling.‖ He
reminds the bishops of Ephesus and the neigh-
bourhood that it is the Holy Ghost who has set
them to govern their churches and feed their flocks.¶
He teaches all the ministers of the Word that it is
impossible for them to preach the Gospel without
being sent by God.**

* "Show whether of these two thou hast chosen"
Acts i. 24).

† "Separate me Saul and Barnabas for the work where-
unto I have taken them " (Acts xiii. 2).

‡ Acts vi. 5.   § Rom. i. 1 ; 1 Cor. i. 1.

‖ "Neither doth man take the honour to himself, but
he that is called by God, as Aaron was" (Heb. v. 4).

¶ "Wherein the Holy Ghost hath placed you bishops to
rule the Church of God" (Act xx. 28).

** "How shall they preach unless they be sent?"
(Rom. x. 15).

The Catholic Church proposes the same doctrine. She is so convinced that God Himself supplies His people with the pastors they need, that from time immemorial she has prescribed the fast and prayers of the Ember-days, in order to obtain from Heaven worthy and holy ministers for the altar. Thus she accomplishes the precept which our Saviour gave her when He said: "The harvest is indeed great, but the labourers are few. Pray ye, therefore, the Lord of the harvest, that He send forth labourers into His harvest."*

The teachings of experience add their weight to the testimony of Holy Writ and the constant practice of the Church. It is evident that if the hand of God had not for eighteen centuries peopled the sanctuary, the ranks of the sacred armament would long since have been exhausted and the succession of the priesthood interrupted. But neither the violence of persecutions, the fury of heresies, the passions of men, the falling-off of the nations, nor even the treachery of some unfaithful ministers—circumstances which ought, in the ordinary course of human affairs, to have quenched the sacred fire of ecclesiastical vocations—have been able to break the chain of the Catholic priesthood, or to dry up in its source the zeal of the priests. Nay, the more pressing have been the wants of the Church, the more generous has the Divine goodness appeared to her. The more difficulties increased, the greater in genius and in holiness were the great men whom God raised up for His people. Pastors have always

* Matt. ix. 37, 38.

been found to rise in the Church, capable of making
head against the storm and superior to fortune ; and
the most learned doctors have always appeared at
the same time as the most powerful heresiarchs.   If
the Divine Pilot of the Church has seemed sometimes to slumber in His bark, it has been to revive
our drowsy zeal and to show forth more strikingly
the resources of His all-powerful goodness in calm-
ing the fury of the waves and guiding the tossed
vessel into harbour by hands which He had formed
and directed Himself.   In the midst of the greatest
dangers, the sacred hierarchy has kept safe the
institutions of the Church, and then especially may
we feel convinced that it is no longer flesh and
blood, as St. Leo puts it, that give birth to the
Pope, but God's grace that creates him.

The causes, in themselves slight and impercep-
tible, which often determine vocations to the ecclesiastical state, furnish a third and, in my opinion,
very convincing proof of God's intervention in these
vocations.   For what do we read in the lives of the
saints ?   That the great St. Antony, when still very
young, one day heard these words of the Gospel
read in Church : " Go sell what thou hast, and give
to the poor, and thou shalt have treasure in heaven."*
These few words, which so many had heard before
him, made an impression on him, and were the beginning of his vocation to the religious state.   St.
Augustine was converted by a simple reading, as
later on was St. Ignatius of Loyola.   These two
great saints afterwards worked immense good in

† Matt. xix. 21.

the Church, and the beginning of their vocation seems all contained in a chance event, as the saying is, of little or no importance. How many great servants of God have devoted themselves to the service of the altar through having heard a heavenly voice speaking in the depths of their heart and inspiring them with an ardent desire to labour for the salvation of souls! We have known holy ecclesiastics, who acknowledged that they had conceived the first idea of their vocation at the sight of a priest decked in his sacred vestments, or after having been charmed by the holy canticles of the Church. For Him who holds the heart of man in His hands, things the most insignificant and inefficacious of themselves become all-powerful instruments. The remarkable disproportion of cause and effect which they produce indicate the operation of that grace which chooses the Pope and creates the priest of God.

Lastly, the sovereign action of God in the choice of His ministers is again shown by the effects that vocation to the ecclesiastical state produces in souls. Humanly speaking, it is impossible for a young man in the flower of his age, and in the presence of the seductions of the world, to renounce joyfully, for natural or human motives, the enjoyments and honours that the world seems to promise him, and for him to exchange these visible joys for the prospect of a humble and mortified life. Nature seeks all that flatters the senses: grace alone inspires the love for things which elevate the soul, ennoble it, and attract it to the beauty of virtue. Under

the reign of worldly ideas, it is impossible to comprehend the holiness, virtue, devotedness, zeal and
self-denial of the priest.   But as soon as we suppose
that it is grace which produces the Pontiff, all these
mysteries are explained and disappear.   We are no
longer astonished that the minister of the altar
abhors the stains of vice and burns with a holy
ardour for virtue : the charm that he finds in his
most painful duties seems quite natural.   When we
see him brave sickness and infection to console one
of his dying brethren, and when we see him, after
the example of the Good Shepherd, even giving his
life for his flock, we admire him, but we are not
surprised, because we are convinced that the finger
of God is there.   The celestial unction which fills
his soul to overflow renders sweet and easy his
roughest labours.   The weight of his obligations,
the bitterness of the outrages he is offered to drink,
the annoyances people try to cause him, the fatigues
of his ministry, the restlessness of his zeal, the privations of his poverty, yield to the empire which
grace exercises over his heart, and only serve to
increase his constancy and merits.   Nature is far
below such prodigies : God alone can work them in
His ministers.   The finger of God is evidently there.
Digitus Dei est hic.

CHAPTER VI.

Vocation to the Ecclesiastical State is both a great honour and a great benefit.

Of all the states of life that Divine Providence has established on earth, the priesthood is, without gainsay, the most noble and the greatest. Whether considered in its origin, or in its aim, or in its prerogatives and functions, nothing but holiness, greatness and sublimity is to be found in it.

If the Son of God, after His Incarnation, had been able to remain on earth till the end of ages in sacred humanity, He would have been the Pontiff and Universal Priest of all the faithful; but before ascending into heaven, to sit at the right hand of His Father, it was necessary for Him to delegate His priesthood to a body of ministers invested with His dignity, authority and powers. It is to replace our Lord Jesus Christ upon earth that God calls chosen souls to the priesthood; it is to continue here below the work of the redemption and sanctification of men, commenced in Bethlehem and consummated on Calvary. It was in this sense that the Apostle, in the name of all the Pontiffs and priests of the Church, said: "For Christ, therefore, we are ambassadors, God, as it were, exhorting by us." * A sublime, a truly celestial mission, which elevates the priests of God above the kings of the

* 2 Cor. v. 20.

earth, above the angels of heaven; a Divine mission,
which assimilates them in some sort to the Son of
God Himself. Only the angels, the prophets, and
the priests of the New Covenant properly bear the
name of ambassadors of Jesus Christ, interpreters of
the Divine oracles and ministers of God. But the
priests rise above the angels and prophets, because
they are not only the envoys of God, but also the
substitutes and lieutenants of His Son.

Moses, according to the Holy Spirit, was the
mediator of the Old Testament: priests, as representing the person of our Saviour, are the mediators
of the New. Jesus Christ, our Divine Master,
dwells in them, works in them, sanctifies us by
them—in a word, accomplishes by their means what
He would have done Himself, had He been able to
remain visibly on earth.

The priesthood, then, has its root in the person of
Jesus Christ: it is born from the necessity of continuing here below the ministry of the God-Saviour.
It has for its end to glorify God by a worship
worthy of Him, to reconcile men with their Maker;
to incessantly unite earth to heaven; to redeem
sinners from the slavery of the devil; to raise up
the just to the honour of Divine sonship; to spread
in the world the light of the Gospel, and to open
all eyes to the faith; to dispense to the children
of men all the sources of grace, and to sanctify
their bodies and souls by the administration of the
Sacraments. The priest is invested with a Divine
authority to combat evil and dispose good; he
condemns sin and commends virtue; by the unction

of his word he heals sick hearts; by the authority
of his ministry he brings back sinners to good, and
leads holy souls in the ways of perfection. He
is father, physician, judge, consoler and sanctifier
in the spiritual order, and really replaces God
Himself upon earth.

To fulfil this sublime mission, God has chosen
him from the midst of His people, and in order
to attach him to Himself He forestalls him by His
grace. He preserves him from the corruption of
the world, and turns him aside from the paths of
vice and error, in order that his heart may become a
pure and holy sanctuary wherein His Divine Majesty
may take pleasure to dwell. The very instant he
receives the sacred unction and becomes a priest
of God, according to the order of Melchisedec, the
elect of God is invested with a miraculous power
which God alone can delegate to the creature. The
Catholic priest has command, in God's name, over
heaven and earth and hell. In the name of Jesus
Christ he opens and closes the gates of heaven
and the gates of hell. The words that, as a priest
of God, he pronounces here below, have their effect
in the home of the blessed or in the home of the
lost. Josue commanded the sun: the priest of
the New Alliance commands God Himself! At his
invitation the Eternal Word descends anew on earth,
veils Himself under the Sacramental Species with as
much love for us as when He hid Himself in the
womb of the Blessed Virgin Mary, under the form
of our weak manhood; and thus, by the hands of
the priest, the Divine Saviour daily immolates Him-

self, in an unbloody manner, to God His Father, for the salvation of the world.

O sublime functions, miraculous power, ineffable dignity of the priesthood! The miracles of man's sanctification are perpetuated here below, only by thee, O priest of God! and if the tradition of the priesthood were to be interrupted, the source of the Divine mercies would be dried up for us, and the order of Providence, which has traced the ways of our salvation, would be upset.

God has not only invested His priests with these truly Divine functions, but He has always over-whelmed them with His love. Even under the Old Law, when the priesthood had not yet attained the degree of sanctity of the Christian priesthood, God took pleasure in the holiness and worthiness of His priests ; and the Holy Spirit, by the mouth of the Royal Prophet, made it one of God's titles to glory that He had Himself raised up His greatest priests ; thus David cried out : "Moses and Aaron among His priests ; and Samuel among them that call upon His name."* What shall we think or say of the dignity of the pontiffs and priests of the New Covenant, elected to replace our Lord Jesus Christ Himself upon earth and invested with powers which reach to the depths of hell and to the highest heavens ?

Happy the souls whom God prepares by His graces for this sublime state ! By raising them to the priesthood He confers on them the greatest

* Ps. xcviii. 6.

dignity that exists on earth, and gives them the greatest honour that He can accord to a creature.

Vocation to the ecclesiastical state is, then, a great honour; it is also a great benefit, whether we consider the grace with which the elect is loaded, or the consolations he obtains, or the merits he acquires.

I have already suggested several times, and further on I will explain more in detail, how God prepares for the priesthood the souls He destines for this holy state. From their earliest age He adorns them with His most efficacious graces and cultivates them by Divine influences, in order that Christian virtues may take root in them and vices be suppressed. He gives them an angel guardian of more elevated rank to watch over their innocency and to draw them away from the snares which the devil and the world set beneath their feet. He obtains for them a Christian education and inspires them with a love of holiness. Fear of the Lord becomes their buckler; zeal for the glory of God and the welfare of their neighbour their sword and helm. They grow in the habit of piety and bear fruit of salvation in due season.

When the glorious day of ordination approaches He redoubles His favours. Then the elect of God enter, in some sort, into a new atmosphere, all impregnated with peace, calm, holiness and joy. They feel their heart growing detached from earth and energetically cleaving to the things of God. Grace works in them in a sensible manner and bears them off to the vestibule of heaven.

Holy transports rise in their hearts and carry
them on towards God. They offer themselves to
Him as victims of sweet savour, and consecrate
to Him for life their bodies, their souls, their
thoughts, feelings, actions—in a word, their whole
person, in order that God may dispose of it according to His good pleasure.

As God the Father prepared the Blessed Virgin
to become the Mother of His Son according to the
flesh, so does He prepare His priests to become the
fathers of His children according to grace. He
sanctifies them Himself, confers on them His most
precious gifts, in order to make them worthy of
the holy state for which He destines them; He
prepares their intellect, their memory, their judgment, all their faculties, in order that they may
serve Him as instruments in the great work of His
mercy; and makes of them men according to His
own heart.

When the elect corresponds to these advances of
grace he makes rapid progress in the way of priestly
perfection, and receives incessantly new favours.
The priest, placed by the fountain-head of all heavenly gifts, draws from it, first and at his own good
pleasure, all the riches that he desires. Dispenser
of all graces, minister of all sanctifications, he has
the right to appropriate to himself the first fruits
and to reserve the flowers of them. Thus we see a
host of God's priests raising themselves, without
effort, to the highest degree of Christian virtues and
spreading in the Church the good odour of Jesus
Christ.

In truth, there is no class of the faithful to
whom God gives so large a share of His supernatural gifts as to His priests. The priests are
the first-born, the 'eldest of His family, His best-
beloved children, the friends of His heart. It
suffices to say that they find in their holy vocation all the graces that a Christian heart can desire
on earth. Hence it also follows that their vocation
is really the greatest benefit that Divine goodness
can impart to them.

This vocation is again a great benefit on account
of the abundant and sweet consolations with which
it inundates the heart.

It is no slight subject of joy for the priest to
see himself chosen by God to replace our Lord
Jesus Christ here below in His Divine function,
consecrated to His service for all his lifetime.
Without speaking of the interior inspirations of
joy which virtue and holiness naturally bring to
the soul, what ineffable joys does the priestly
ministry procure!

What a happiness for the priest to increase
without ceasing the people of God, by receiving
into the Church the children whom he regenerates
by Baptism! What a joy to thus beget new sons
to Jesus Christ! Father and shepherd of souls,
he watches anxiously over the lambs and preserves
them from the wolf's fangs. He sees the flock
committed to him grow in virtue and piety. Repentant sinners come and cast themselves at his
feet, which they water with their tears, and beg
from him pardon of their sins. Who can tell all

the joy that the minister of God feels when he is
called to close the gates of hell for these penitent
souls and to open for them the gates of heaven?—
when he sees hearts, long grown hard, suddenly
transformed by a miracle of grace and eagerly
setting forth on the path of virtue? The priest
feels that he possesses in himself a Divine strength
which makes his feeble efforts powerful, and crowns
in a wondrous manner his slightest labours. These
successes encourage him, uphold him and make him
superior to all obstacles. Hence it is that the
rudest shocks cannot shake his resolutions nor
bend his will.

The more exalted in dignity the priest is, the
more exposed is he to the winds of tribulation.
Hell, which cannot prevail against the Church,
has still the power to wage war against her. The
kingdom of God suffers violence; and the minister
of God is often the first to undergo the attacks
which the enemies of good direct against God's
work. These attacks cannot disturb the happiness
of the priest who is faithful to his vocation, but
they complete and perfect it, because he is always
ready, thanks to the Divine strength with which he
feels inspired, to cry out with the Apostle, "I exceedingly abound with joy in all our tribulation."*

What shall I say of the joy that fills the priest's
heart when he offers the Sacred Mysteries, whilst
the court of heaven all about him adores the Sacramental God Whom he carries in his hands? What

* 2 Cor. vii. 4.

shall I say, again, of the place that is reserved for
the priest at the Last Judgment in the heart of the
heavenly Jerusalem ? All these joys and consolations are included in the ecclesiastical vocation, as
the tree in its root, the shrub in its seed. Is it
not then correct to say that this vocation is a
distinguished benefit on the part of God?

Vocation to the ecclesiastical state is, moreover, a
fruitful source of merit. All the faithful can, doubtless, amass treasures for heaven by consecrating
to the service of God the days and hours that He
has reserved to Himself. The heavenly Jerusalem
reckons among its citizens persons from every rank
of the faithful. Immense is the number of lay-folk
who merit heaven by their good works. Nevertheless we must acknowledge that the lot of the priest
is, in this respect, far superior to that of the ordinary
faithful. Most men consecrate the greater part of
their time and strength to worldly business, the
wants of their body, the needs of either family or
state. Priests can devote themselves entirely to
the things of heaven, the wants of souls, and the
great affair of salvation. The hours that the
ordinary faithful employ in exercising an art or
trade, or a public duty, the priest employs in
adoring God, saving souls, and sanctifying himself.
Whatever occupation he may have, the priest never
quits the supernatural sphere in which his vocation
has placed him ; consequently, he never loses the
opportunity of pleasing God, doing good works, and
increasing the store of his merits. All that the law
of God requires from him, all that the faithful

expect from him, all that the Church demands.
from him, or imposes on him—all tends to sanctify
him, to make him well-pleasing to God, and to
secure him an eternal reward.

Vocation to the ecclesiastical state, which procures him this advantage, is, therefore, a great
benefit, and the Christian who obtains it should.
think himself the happiest of men.

But, as we have already said, everybody is not
called to the priesthood. God does not grant this
benefit to all men: "He hath not done in like
manner to every nation;"* and it is not allowable
to thrust oneself into this holy state without being
formally called thereunto. Before engaging in it
we must make sure of God's will, which is ordinarily
manifested by sensible signs. Let us then examine
by what signs a Christian youth may recognize
God's will concerning himself.

CHAPTER VII.

Of the Signs of Vocation to the Ecclesiastical State..

GOD has spoken at divers times and in divers
manners to men, first of Himself, then by His prophets, and lastly by His Divine Son. He made
His voice heard in the earthly Paradise without
surrounding it with the dazzling and awful adorn--

* Ps. cxlvii. 20.

ments of His Majesty. He spake to Moses amid thunder and lightning; He manifested Himself to the prophets in dreams and visions; He still converses daily with His Church by the inspirations of His Divine Spirit, Who teaches and suggests to her all truth.

But this speaking is extraordinary. God employs in regard to us a manner of speaking more suited to our weakness, and more conformable to the ordinary and common laws of His providence: I mean to say that He speaks by the events He directs, by the qualities He confers, by the laws and decrees of the Church that He inspires. Such is the language by which He is accustomed to designate the ministers of His altar.

The ordinary signs of vocation to the ecclesiastical state are those found within our reach. We do not hear God's voice, as Samuel did in the Temple; nor as St. Paul on the road to Damascus; but we observe the manifestations of His will in the natural and supernatural gifts which He grants us. the intellectual and moral qualities with which He has endowed us, the will of the superiors to whose care He entrusts us, the events He causes to take place around us.

The signs of heavenly vocation are of two kinds: some interior and, so to speak, personal; others exterior and dependent on divers circumstances. Generally, we must believe a young man called to the ecclesiastical state, who manifestly possesses, together with a taste for this state, the necessary fitness and qualities to sustain its obligations and

fulfil the duties of it, and who meets no obstacle to
embracing it.   Divine Providence is supposed to
call to these sublime functions all Christian youths
whom it has rendered fit to acquit themselves of
them, and for whom it seems to make smooth all
the paths of the sanctuary.   This fitness and
capacity, so rare in a high degree, are never granted
to young men without some providential purpose.
They indicate, therefore, Heaven's will, and are its
interpreters. As few young men possess this sum of
qualities which forestall all doubts, it is necessary
to note in this place those which deserve most
attention, and which may be considered, even when
isolated, as signs of Divine vocation to the ecclesiastical state.

I. The first sign is *purity of intention.*

When a young man, presenting himself to embrace the ecclesiastical state, has no other motive
than God's glory, the welfare of souls, and his own
sanctification; when he is moved by the fear of
danger in the world, by horror of vice and love of
virtue ; moreover, if, in order to enter the ecclesiastical state, he makes material sacrifices, such
as renouncing an easy position in the world ;
and, besides, is of ordinary capacity—we must
believe that this young man is called by God to
the ecclesiastical state.

II. The second sign is a *marked taste* for this
state.

I mean to speak of a young man who, from
earliest infancy, or, at least, from coming to the
use of reason, has felt the desire to consecrate him-

self to God and to the service of the altar, and has
felt this desire increase with his age, notwithstanding the distractions and temptations he has gone
through.   I suppose that the ceremonies of Divine
worship have for him a peculiar charm ; that the
sight of God's ministers inspires him with a sentiment of respectful joy ; and that all that regards
the ministry of the altar has for him a particular
attraction.   If this inclination—supposing it to be,
moreover, combated from time to time by rising
passions, or to have grown tepid through worldly
thoughts, or been overcast by momentary doubts
—if this inclination perseveres, from early childhood until youth, the time in which we determine the choice of our state of life, I have no fear
in saying that it is a manifest sign of vocation to
the ecclesiastical state.

III. The third sign is great *innocency of life*
and perfect purity of heart.

Among the children who receive in their own
families, and in our colleges, a solid and really
Christian education, we meet a great number who
preserve their innocence to a very advanced age.
They know not evil, and love good alone; they
observe God's commandments with simplicity; they
are acquainted with neither the malice of the
world nor the scandal of disorders.   Grace reigns
in their soul, and preserves there all the brightness
of heavenly purity.*

* " My readers may be assured that a Catholic boy, as
such, is generally a different species of being from a Protestant boy. He frequently preserves his innocence, his

F

It is certain that God takes pleasure in these
souls which preserve His image so perfectly, and
never sadden the Holy Ghost. God formerly
claimed the first-born of His people, and the first-
fruit of all that the earth produced, as the most
excellent gift that could be made to Him. In like
manner, without doubt, he chooses as ornaments
for His Church these pure souls which the devil has
never seduced, which sin has never soiled, and in
which the Holy Spirit has ever dwelt. " Blessed
are the clean of heart," says the Gospel, " for they
shall see God." * To see God and to be looked
upon with pleasure by Him is the privilege of
virgins and of innocent hearts. This quality, considering the great number of children whose innocence is sullied at an early age, is so uncommon,
even rare; it is, moreover, so proper for the priesthood, whose essence is, so to speak, perfect purity
of body and soul, that it seems it is preserved by
Providence in such a high degree in these chosen
souls, only to prepare them for the ministry of the
altar and the special service of God. This perfect
innocency, if other essential qualities are not want-

simplicity, his openness and guilelessness of character, to
an extent which I believe to be wholly without parallel
among the best of Protestants. And at this very time I
am convinced that there are large numbers of grown up
Catholics in this country, especially among the priesthood,
who have retained the freshness of their baptismal purity,
and who know sin as a matter of *knowledge* only, and not
of experience."—(*Four Year's Experience of the Catholic
Religion.* By J. MOORE CAPES, pp. 60-3. London: 1849.)
This observation is very just and very correct.
                    * Matt. v. 8.

ing, is therefore a certain sign of vocation to the ecclesiastical state.

Happy the young men who have preserved their baptismal innocence during their early life! At the same time we must be careful not to think that this perfect innocency is absolutely necessary for taking upon oneself the burden of the priesthood. A sect, which has drawn away more souls from God by their excessive rigour than all the casuists in the world by their extreme indulgence, pretended that without baptismal innocence it is not allowable to enter into Holy Orders; but this maxim, so discouraging to the numberless souls who have sincerely turned back to God, has been smitten by the anathema of the Holy See, which has ever admitted to Holy Orders innocence, whether intact or restored.* If we see even on our altars and around God's throne saints of both sexes, who, after having been sinners, have practised virtue to an heroic degree; if grace often abounds where iniquity has abounded, it is evident that ecclesiastical vocation is compatible with an unfortunate past generously atoned for. It is for directors to judge whether the old wounds are healed, evil habits corrected, whether virtue has at last recovered sufficient sway over the soul to dissipate the fears that the future may inspire.

* Pius VI., in the celebrated bull "*Auctorem Fidei*," published December 1, 1786, condemns the 53rd proposition of the Jansenist Council of Pistoja, which stigmatizes, as an abuse contrary to the apostolic discipline, the custom of admitting to Holy Orders those of the faithful who have not preserved their baptismal innocence. St. Matthew, the publican, who was considered a public sinner, was called to the apostleship, notwithstanding his sins.

IV. A fourth sign of vocation to the ecclesiastical state is a *sincere love of Jesus*.

This sign is pointed out to us by our Saviour Himself. On the point of definitely confiding to St. Peter the supreme Pontificate of His Church, He addressed to him twice over these touching words: "Simon, son of John, lovest thou me more than these?" and Peter answered Him: "Lord, Thou knowest that I love Thee." Then the Divine Master said to him: "Feed my lambs, feed my sheep." * Jesus Christ says not to Peter, Art thou more prudent, more zealous, more learned, more courageous, more able than thy brethren? He only asks him this one question: "Lovest thou me more?" And when His love had been verified He entrusted to him at once His lambs and sheep, that is to say, all his flock.

What is the meaning of this conduct of our Saviour, except that love to Jesus Christ is the peculiar virtue of pastors, and that to possess it to a certain degree is to bear in oneself a manifest sign of vocation to this sublime charge?

If a young man is burning with a sincere love for Jesus Christ, and constantly feeding these Divine flames in the depths of his heart; if the most touching mysteries of the life of the God-Saviour, such as the Child Jesus in the cradle, God the Consecrator in the Upper Room, God the Redeemer on Calvary, —touch him, move him, transport him out of himself, and force from his soul the cry: "Yea, Lord, Thou knowest that I love Thee!"—if he feels a great

* John xxi. 15—17.

attraction for Holy Communion and often visits the Blessed Sacrament hidden in our tabernacles, then, indeed, you cannot doubt that this young man is called to the ecclesiastical state, for God draws and binds him to Himself by very sensible bonds.

V. A fifth sign of vocation to the ecclesiastical state is *great zeal for the welfare of souls.*

Our Lord Jesus Christ came down from Heaven for us and for our salvation. " I am come to cast fire on the earth," saith He, "and what will I but that it be kindled?" *

Such is the type of the elect to the priesthood.

That youth is truly called to this holy state who burns with the desire of sacrificing himself for the salvation of men and of becoming like the Apostle, " anathema for his brethren." † The fire which quickens him may be compared to the live coals which purified the lips of Isaias ‡ and prepared them to announce God's Word. The fields white to harvest § have struck his eye; he has asked the Master of the House to be allowed to be reckoned among the labourers who gather in His sheaves, and God accepts him in the ranks of His faithful servants. The sight of so many sinners ignoring and violating God's rights pierces his generous soul with a sword of sorrow; the misfortune of so many unhappy ones who know not the time of their visitation ‖ ; the fury of the Prince of Darkness and his numberless satellites, far from sinking his courage or checking

---

* Luke xii. 49. † Rom. ix. 3. ‡ Is. vi. 7—9.
§ John iv. 35. ‖ Luke xix. 44.

his enthusiasm, inspire him with a more ardent
desire to enter the lists with the enemies of God
and the Church and stir him up to engage in the
battle.

Zeal for the salvation of souls is also shown in a
youthful heart by frequent and continued aspirations
to the Catholic apostleship, whether amid the Christian nations of Europe or amid the infidels and
idolators of far-off countries.   He who despises the
comforts of life, the dreams of ambition, the sheen
of honour, the whirl of pleasure, who thinks only of
repairing the offences committed against the Divine
Majesty, and of establishing the reign of piety and
virtue ; he who, perhaps, aspires to cross seas, scale
mountains, and break all obstacles, in order to carry
the light of faith to peoples still sitting in the
shadow of death : this young man is truly animated
with the spirit which makes the priests of God—
he is certainly called to the priesthood.

If the desire of martyrdom is joined to the other
inspirations of zeal, the call of Heaven acquires a
new degree of certainty.

At this point I must be allowed to forestall a
possible mistake.

People sometimes imagine that young men of a
violent or irascible character are not called to a
priesthood which breathes nothing but peace and
mildness.   Still this character is not always a sign
of non-vocation.   It may, doubtless, be so when the
young man who is affected by it has very little
virtue, feels no desire to overcome himself, and
makes no effort to tame his natural impetuosity.

But with virtuous youths this innate ardour, this impatience, in some sort identified with the blood, if it is held in bonds by reason and overruled by virtue, may become the principle of many great deeds, and give them a fitness for a life all of zeal, at which vulgar souls never arrive. The heroism of the apostleship is the snare of souls of a strong temperament. Vigorous characters formed under the influence of grace are capable of the most noble enterprizes, and often obtain astonishing successes. They have a great power of making beginnings and are especially fitted to command. St. Francis Xavier, the great Apostle of the Indies, is a striking example of the wonders God sometimes works by the ministry of courageous, ardent, and powerful men, who unite a docile will to an impetuous heart.

Thus when an ardent soul keeps itself steady in the love of virtue, even amid dangers which appear likely to carry it away—when, moreover, it is gifted with a delicate conscience, and eagerly takes up the yoke of God, to whom it longs to consecrate all its strength, we may rest assured that, notwithstanding its natural hotness of temper, this soul is called to serve God in the sacred ministry and to work for the salvation of souls.

VI. A sixth sign of vocation is manifested in a great *esteem for ecclesiastical functions* and an ardent desire of practising them.

We may sometimes notice among children a particular attraction for the ceremonies of the Church and for all that concerns the Divine Service. They love to busy themselves with altars, with the orna-

ments and vessels of the Church, to take part in
the offices, and sing the hymns of God. The sacred
rites charm, captivate them : they find a particular
attraction in them. This inclination is not a thing
of chance, it gives us a mark impossible to overlook
when inquiring what may be God's will with regard
to such a soul.

VII. A seventh sign of vocation to the ecclesiastical state shows itself in a *sincere and lively love
of priestly perfection*, and in frequent aspirations
to the most exalted virtues.

A heart quickened with a very lively fear of the
Lord, with a profound aversion for vice and a constant horror of sin, is evidently under the empire
of a special grace, and feels itself spontaneously
carried on towards a state from which God has
removed most of the spiritual dangers that are met
with in the world, towards a state to which He has
attached an infinitude of graces in order to preserve
those who embrace it. This love of perfection is,
therefore, a prognostication, the meaning of which
is quite certain.

It would be easy to add to these principal signs
other manifestations, more or less sensible, of the
Divine will; but these details are not necessary
here. The Spirit of God and the experience of a
wise director will supply for all. Provided that
you open your heart and your ears to grace, grace
will easily succeed in making itself understood.

Still, to complete the explanations which we have
just given of the *inward* signs of Divine vocation to
the ecclesiastical state, we must say something

about the *outward* signs by which Divine Providence is from time to time pleased to manifest
His will.

There are two principal outward signs: first, the
desire of the people and the needs of the Church;
next, the judgment of lawful superiors.

I. There is a saying, *Vox populi, vox Dei*, and
in many remarkable cases this proverb has been
verified to the letter. So history tells us that the
people of Milan, after the death of their Arian
bishop, not being able to agree about the election of
a new pastor, the prefect of the province sent one of
his magistrates, named Ambrose, to appease the
tumult and bring back peace among the faithful.
As he sent him, he said to him, "Act as a bishop,
rather than as a judge." Ambrose obeyed, and
spoke to the people with such unction, that he
calmed their passions and inspired them with a
desire for peace. Whilst he was yet speaking, a
child cried out, "Ambrose for bishop!" And the
people, regarding the cry as an admonition from
Heaven, in their turn cried out, "Ambrose for
bishop!" The Emperor, informed of these circumstances, ratified the election of Ambrose, who thus
became Bishop of Milan and one of the lights of
the Church.

We read in the life of St. Paulinus of Nola that,
when still young, he was forced by the people of
Barcelona to receive the priesthood, and afterwards
exercised it to the great edification of the whole
Church.

St. John Chrysostom, who had constantly refused

the charge of the episcopate, was led by a pious
stratagem to accept it.   He could not resist the
will of God manifested in that of His people.

St. Gregory the Great, having taken to flight to
escape the honours of the Papacy, Heaven itself
betrayed his retreat by miraculous signs, and the
great servant of God was obliged, by the unanimous
voice of clergy and people, to accept the heavy
burden.

In these and other like circumstances Divine
vocation is manifested by the desires of the people,
without leaving any doubt of its meaning.

II. We must also consider, as a certain sign of
vocation to the ecclesiastical state, the judgment of
lawful pastors who have received from God a special
grace to choose their clerics and to perpetuate their
priesthood in the midst of the faithful.

Our Divine Saviour, whose lieutenants are the
bishops on earth, commenced by Himself choosing
His numerous disciples, from among whom He afterwards picked out His twelve Apostles.   The Gospel
narrates with particular care the circumstances of
this election, in order to teach us that it was a
Divine act, the execution of which our Saviour
reserved to Himself. Although this was evident from
the very circumstances which had presided over
the election, still the Holy Spirit willed that the
Gospel should preserve for us the words in which
our Divine Saviour recalled this remarkable fact to
the Apostles themselves. " You have not chosen me,"
says He to them, " but I have chosen you."*   Our

* John xv. 16.

Heavenly Master wished to show us by this that
bishops should in aftertime choose their clerics and
priests, and transmit to them, in the name of Jesus
Christ, whose place they hold, the powers of the
priesthood and the Divine mission.

In his letters to Timothy and Titus, St. Paul
often recalls to his disciples, and consequently to all
bishops, the rule of their duty in the choice of God's
ministers; he recommends them not to raise neophytes to the priesthood, nor to impose hands with
too great precipitation; he explains to them the
qualities necessary for bishops and priests to exercise the priesthood worthily and with fruit. We
see that the Apostle is thoroughly penetrated with
the importance of these elections which God directs
by His Spirit, but the care of which has been left
to the chiefs of His Church. Bishops have always
understood the importance of this duty, and have
always fulfilled it with great solicitude. As judges
of vocations which are manifested under the influence of Divine grace in the midst of the faithful,
they have ever summoned to themselves those
whom the Holy Spirit pointed out for their choice,
and driven from the sanctuary those who would
invade it uncalled of God.

The judgment of the bishops in the matter of
ecclesiastical vocation is, therefore, quite decisive.
We may say that it serves as a rule, as a check,
upon all the other signs of God's will that we have
enumerated. When the bishop calls, God calls;
when the bishop refuses, it is God Himself who
refuses. His sentence must prevail over all indi-

vidual signs, and it alone can supply for all signs. You are certain not to be mistaken if you follow this voice and accept this evidence.

We have now explained the principal signs of vocation to the ecclesiastical state. We must now make known the signs of non-vocation, for it often happens that a young man finds in himself motives to believe that he is called, and other motives which lead him to believe that he is not called. How, then, can he listen to and compare these apparently contradictory reasons, if he has not learnt to discriminate their origin and worth?

Hence, let us briefly examine what, in a young man deliberating on the choice of a state of life, are the signs of non-vocation to the ecclesiastical state, and what conclusions we may lawfully draw from them.

CHAPTER VIII.

Of the signs of Non-Vocation to the Ecclesiastical State.

We may, first of all, establish this general rule : that every young man deprived of the qualities necessary, according to the laws of the Church, for receiving Holy Orders and exercising the priestly ministry, is not called of God to the ecclesiastical state. When God calls a person to a special state, He begins by making him fit for that state, by endowing him with suitable faculties and furnishing him with the means of bearing its burdens and fulfilling its duties. The absence of one or two other qualities necessary to the priest for fulfilling his functions is a certain sign of non-vocation.

It is not less certain that a young man, subject to vices altogether contrary to priestly virtues, affected by notable and sensible defects, attacked by grave infirmity or corporal deformity, which render him incapable of exercising ecclesiastical functions with dignity and decency, is not called to the priesthood, and bears in these vices, defects or deformities, a certain sign of non-vocation.

In order better to grasp the tendency of these two general rules, let us enter into details and distinguish these signs of non-vocation into *intrinsic* or personal, and *extrinsic* or circumstantial ones.

Intrinsic or personal signs of non-vocation are of three sorts : vices of the mind, of the heart, of the body. Such is the plan on which our observations are arranged.

I. I say, first of all, that *vices of the mind* are 'signs of non-vocation to the ecclesiastical state. I will signalize those that deserve special attention.

We may reckon in the first rank, amid the defects excluding from the priesthood, a profound, natural and well-nigh invincible *ignorance*.

The Holy Spirit marks out knowledge among the first qualities of a priest, when He says that the people shall seek knowledge from the lips of the priest. * Our Divine Saviour has, so to speak, summed up the whole mission of His Apostles and

---

* Malach. ii. 7.

their successors when He said to them: "Go and teach." The priest is essentially a teacher in the midst of the faithful : the aspirant to the priesthood must, therefore, possess a certain aptitude for study, and be capable of teaching the truths of faith to the souls entrusted to him. A young man of blind and obtuse mind is not capable of fulfilling these duties: he is marked with the stamp of those souls who are called to ordinary life : he is not called to the priesthood.

This does not mean that, in order to rise to Holy Orders, he must possess a vast and deep mind, or have acquired very extensive knowledge. No: the Church, it is true, should always count in her midst some men of superior knowledge, capable of giving account of their faith, and of putting to silence whosoever sets himself up against the science of God. Such men have never been wanting to her. She has always possessed doctors, powerful in word and teaching, whenever hell has raised up powerful foes against her; but the supereminent qualities of these chiefs of God's people are not the ordinary share of aspirants to the priesthood. An ordinary intelligence is sufficient for most of these aspirants to answer the views of Providence concerning them. Experience has even proved that subjects, moderate as regards intellectual faculties, but filled with piety, zeal and prudence, often succeed in the pastoral ministry much better than subjects endowed with brilliant talents. Whether it be that the vanity of these latter checks the effects of grace, or that God takes pleasure, as He did around the cradle of His Church, in confounding the strong by the weak, and proving that His gifts are independent of the arts of human eloquence, and often follow in preference the eloquence of the heart and the practice of priestly virtues, we often see humble and modest ecclesiastics achieve greater successes than those who, in respect of talents and knowledge, appear far superior to them.

We must also pay attention to the position of the subject. An ecclesiastic gifted with great piety, who enjoys an honourable subsistence, and who desires to instruct and edify his brethren by his example and virtue much more than by his words, may be admitted to Orders even when his intellectual faculties are not brilliant.

The Church also demands less from religious who are placed in the cloister, and may there exercise many priestly functions, independently of very extensive learning.

The remarks we have offered especially concern young men who aspire to the functions of the sacred ministry in parishes, i.e., to the pastoral ministry. This vocation evidently supposes an open mind, moderate faculties, and a certain aptitude for study. A rooted ignorance is, therefore, for these candidates, a sign of non-vocation.

Secondly, I call *singularity*, especially in matters of piety, a vice of the mind. St. Francis of Sales had such a dread of singular and eccentric minds, that he constantly refused to ordain them. He feared less certain weaknesses of the heart, generously atoned for, than affectation of extraordinary devotion, the passion for making oneself remarkable, eccentricities of behaviour, studied humility joined to pleasure in speaking of self, strange manners, exorbitant zeal for trifling things, a mind critical and sarcastic of others, and excessively indulgent to self. Such characters are never compatible with the functions of the priesthood. One who has not succeeded in correcting himself of them is ignorant of the very first principles of true devotion. A piety according to God's heart does not take up these whims. It applies itself, first and foremost, to the fulfilment of the ordinary duties of life, loves modesty and simplicity, respects common rules, never makes itself remarkable by eccentricities and freaks, but by the order and regularity of its movements. Even these saints, whom God has led by extraordinary paths to the higher degrees of contemplation, have passed through the inferior degrees and the ordinary paths of Christian perfection. And, indeed, it is not at an age when we have to deliberate on the choice of a state of life that we can hope to have already gone through these ordinary paths. Singularity in matters of piety in young people always, therefore, indicates oddities of mind which, in the last analysis, are resolved into disgust for essential duties or the freaks of a blind and inconstant piety.

A very pronounced tendency to *scruples* is also a sign of non-vocation to the ecclesiastical state. This disposition is a real sickness of the mind, whose cure is excessively difficult, and into which relapses are only natural in a state where the

obligations and duties are all, for timid souls, a
natural subject of disquiet and perplexity.

The scrupulous man fears where there is no room
for fear : for him everything is a subject of hesitation and regret. His duties, whether performed or
omitted, are an inexhaustible source of imaginary
faults. Everything that presents itself to him as a
duty is only seen through the prism of his uneasy
disposition. Consequently the good advice that is
given him, instead of assisting him, embarrasses him
and gives rise to new difficulties. He is like those
sick people whose stomachs are so weak that they
can bear neither food nor medicines. Beneath the
weight of the priesthood this evil is in some sort
incurable. Moreover, a person who is not in a fit
state to direct himself, nor to accept for himself
the direction of another, how can he become a good
guide for God's people ? I have no fear in saying
that minds thoroughly scrupulous should be removed from the sanctuary, in order to preserve them
from folly in this world and from a very sad fate
in the next.

Hypocrisy, or two-facedness, considered as a
characteristic quality, is also a vice very contrary
to the holiness of the ecclesiastical state. Jesus
Christ, who calls all His ministers to follow His
footsteps, calls Himself the "Truth." He recommends to them the simplicity of the dove united
with the prudence of the serpent : He smote with
anathema the two-facedness of the Pharisees, whom
He styled "whited sepulchres." The chastisement
of Ananias and Sapphira warns false and lying souls

G

of what God has in store for them when they impose upon His Church. Young men of this character are not called to the functions of the priesthood.

Pride, well developed and domineering over the mind, is another impediment to the ecclesiastical state. Pride is the vice that drove Lucifer from heaven, and Adam from Paradise. It has been the principal of all the heresies that have afflicted the Church and of all the schisms that have wounded her charity. This vice, when carried to a certain degree, destroys the spirit of subordination, which is the bond of the ecclesiastical hierarchy; it leads to the rigour and inflexibility which make a superior unbearable to his subordinates; it leads to presumption, which is incompatible with prudence; it hurries into disputes and quarrels, which are contrary to charity and to the spirit of the Church, according to that of the Apostle: " If any man seem to be contentious, we have no such custom nor the Church of God." * A proud spirit would find dangerous food for his pride in the dignity of the ecclesiastical state, and in the respect with which his character would be honoured. The proud, like Lucifer, always end in a fall; we have a contemporary example in a celebrated priest who might have been a subject of glory for the Church, but who has become a subject of shame and grief for her.

If, then, we meet with a young man puffed up with vanity, pretentious, full of self, quarrelsome,

---

* 1 Cor. xi. 16.

disliking obedience, indocile to superiors, harsh to inferiors, intolerant of all criticism, but criticising everybody; we may say, without fear of mistake, that he has not the spirit of Jesus Christ, and that he is not called to the priesthood. He who knows not how to obey is not fit to command; he who knows not how to submit is not made to rule. "But the servant of the Lord," saith St. Paul, "must not wrangle: but be mild towards all men, apt to teach, patient, with modesty admonishing them that resist the truth; if, peradventure, God may give them repentance to know the truth, and they may recover themselves from the snares of the devil, by whom they are held captive at his will."* A haughty and proud spirit is incapable of ever observing this precept of the Apostle.

II. We next come to *vices of the heart.*

The most dangerous of all is that which, together with pride, is innate in all of us, as an heirloom from our first parent: sensuality.

A young man who has been given to the vice of impurity, if he has to reproach himself with grave falls and inveterate habits, ranks among those who understand not and will never understand the counsel of Jesus Christ, which every priest must faithfully follow. The tyranny of this vice over those who have become its slaves is terrible. Besides, nothing appears more contrary to the holiness of the priesthood than the stain of this bondage, which degrades the soul, blunts good sentiments,

* 2 Tim. ii. 24—26.

and completely destroys all relish for the things of God.

We will not enter into further details. It is for directors to look, before God, for what they may hope or what they must fear in each particular case. Without doubt, when the wounds are not deep nor old, when the will is powerful and graces appear abundant, all hope of cure is not lost. But the Sacred Canons reasonably exact that he who takes up the yoke of the priesthood must no longer be the slave of this shameful vice; they would have him perfectly free, with that freedom of the children of God which, with the help of grace, makes virtue dear and easy.*

Avarice, which often shows itself in children, is also a sign of non-vocation. This was the dominant vice and cause of the ruin of Judas, the first apostate whom we meet under the New Law. The avaricious man is inaccessible to charity, the first of Christian virtues, and the most necessary quality of a pastor. Jesus Christ said that men should recognize His disciples by the love they showed one to another: the avaricious man is not to be known by this mark, for he is always hard and immovable, always an egotist, always a worshipper of temporal goods.

Idleness and *indolence* also constitute a serious impediment to the ecclesiastical vocation. An apa-

---

* You may consult St. Alfonso de' Liguori, who has written a special dissertation on this delicate question, and also the learned Hallier, in his excellent work of *Sacred Elections and Ordinations.*

thetic character will never make the talent fructify which the Master has entrusted to him; but he will bury it, like the unfaithful servant of whom the Gospel tells us; he will not pluck up the cockle which is choking the good seed; like to the hireling, who takes to flight at the approach of the hungry wolf, he will let his sheep and lambs be worried, instead of protecting and defending them.

Inconstancy, which is generally united to a great *fickleness* of character, is a constant danger of falling, in a steadfast, permanent and perpetual state, whose obligations are numerous and whose contests with hell are incessant. It will be sufficient for us to have pointed out this vice, whose sad results in a minister of God every one can easily apprehend.

But of all the signs which render an apparent vocation suspicious, there is none more striking than a purely *human intention*, based on temporal motives. As soon as a young man, with full knowledge of the case, or even deceiving himself, says in his heart, or by his conduct, "Let us possess the sanctuary of God for an inheritance,"* we may be assured that he is not called of God, but urged by hunger, pride, or ambition.†

In order to discriminate easily the upright and pure intentions of a young man truly called, from the interested intentions of him who is not called,

* Ps. lxxxii. 13.
† " He who seeks by means of the clerical office anything else except God, is neither chosen of God, nor doth he choose God " (Ivo Carnot, Sermon "Of the Excellence of Holy Order.")

we must distinguish three manners of considering the advantages presented by the ecclesiastical state. This state offers considerable spiritual advantages, but in the eyes of man it also promises honours, authority, and livelihood.

He who considers in this state only the spiritual advantages attached to it, such as more abundant graces, more opportunities of labouring for one's salvation, and who puts aside altogether the rest, ranks among the perfect.

He who, whilst appreciating and desiring the spiritual advantages of the ecclesiastical state, allows himself to be influenced by the desire of temporal advantages, which he considers as second-ary and accessory motives, does no injury to the Divine Law.

But they who consider in the ecclesiastical state its temporal advantages only, and who, conse-quently, act as if the kingdom of God consisted in eating and drinking, which the Apostle expressly forbids,* can only enter the ecclesiastical state through the window, like robbers and thieves.

But how can you convince yourself that you only desire to enter this state for temporal motives?

The thing is not difficult. Examine, firstly, whether temporal motives alone present themselves almost always to your mind; next, whether the desire which these motives excite is lively, disturb-ing, sometimes violent; thirdly, whether this desire has been fostered by you for a long time deliber-

---

* Rom. xiv. 17.

ately, and in the hopes of leading an easy, perhaps
dissipated life. Fourthly, whether the principal
object or aim of this desire is a thing of great importance, *e.g.*, the alteration of your position, or a
considerable amelioration of that of your family.
Fifthly, whether, in order to arrive at the priesthood, you are ready to employ all means, even
somewhat indelicate ones, which you have in your
power, such as promises, presents, threats, hypocrisy, the influence of great people, simony. And
if, after this examination, you find that you are in
some points in this condition, do not hesitate to
believe that it is not God, but flesh and blood which
call you to the priesthood, and renounce it without
delay. Jesus Christ, who reproached the crowd
with following Him only to obtain from Him their
food,* will reproach you on the judgment-day with
having yielded to those deceitful words of the devil:
"All these," that is, "all the kingdoms of the world
and the glory of them, will I give thee, if falling
down thou wilt adore me."†

But is the danger of entering into the ecclesiastical state for temporal motives to be feared
nowadays for youth, when the Church has been
stripped of her honours and goods—nowadays when
the clergy are almost everywhere rejected and
persecuted?

Yes, without the least doubt, this danger is to
be feared; experience has fully demonstrated it.
Although the Church has lost her ancient riches

* John vi. 26.   † Matt. iv. 8, 9.

and public honours, she still preserves, thanks to
Divine Providence, means of existence for her ministers, and a general esteem, both capable of tempt-
ing vulgar ambition and drawing aside many hearts.

But if you exclude from the priesthood young
men subject to pride, ambition and sensuality, you
must exclude everybody, for these vices, sad heirloom from our first parent, are found to a certain
degree in all men.

It is true that all men carry in themselves a
fund of pride and sensuality which springs from
original sin, but all are not ruled by these vices
to the extent of being their slaves.   These evil
inclinations are for all men a source of wrestling
and contests, but they are not for all the foundation of a shameful slavery which absorbs the faculties and destroys the energy for good.   We can
conceive a young man who, tempted by these vices,
succeeds in overcoming them by the help of grace,
and in gaining in the contest against them strength
and courage.   But there are others who take up
the yoke without being able to break its chains,
or of ever gaining that sway over self which is
essential to virtue.   It is of these latter that we
spoke, when we said that their vices are a sign of
non-vocation.   If the Church were only to receive
among her pastors souls exempt from all fault and
all imperfection, the gates of the sanctuary would
have to be closed upon the children of men, and the
priestly functions could only be entrusted to angels
come down from heaven.   The solidest virtue does
not shut out every evil inclination, every tempta-

tion, every struggle; on the contrary, it supposes them, for it properly consists in ease in fighting our enemies, and surmounting the obstacles that hell opposes to us.

What we wished to say is reducible to this principle: that souls deeply infected with a capital vice, and ruled by almost incurable evil habits, are not called to the priesthood.

But since it is not necessary to have acquired great virtues before entering the ecclesiastical state, wherefore is it necessary to have uprooted these great vices?

The reason is very clear. Young persons who carry in their heart nascent virtues will easily, with the help of grace, nourish and develope them, until they become solidly virtuous; and, notwithstanding certain defects and weaknesses, they are on the highroad to great virtues. But those who, at the age for choosing a state of life, are already subjugated by a vice that domineers over them and holds them in bondage, are exposed to the danger of bearing their yoke all the days of their life; they have but slight chance of soon getting the better of it, and of arriving at that perfect liberty of the children of God which is the portion of true virtue. In this state of spiritual infirmity a young man can have no hope of one day combating successfully the vices of others, nor of serving the Church as a faithful minister. He must choose the common life, and employ therein for his sanctification the ordinary means of salvation.

But are untamable vices and inclinations so very

perverse ever met with in young souls? Are not
these sad maladies the portion of fully developed
men?

Alas! we must confess that great vices are often
to be found at an age when we rarely meet with
great virtues. This is one of the sad consequences
of original sin. It is not less certain that young
men infected with these vices sometimes present
themselves at the gates of the sanctuary in order to
be received therein. We must keep watch, therefore, at the entrance of the Temple of the Lord to
exclude therefrom the "profane," that is to say, all
those who are swayed by violent passions, inveterate
habits, and faults which we may call incorrigible.
For how can those who are under the empire of
such dispositions believe themselves called to lead
others into the paths of salvation, and to direct
them therein, when they themselves have not
entered them, and when, notwithstanding the grace
which assists them thereto, they know not how to
keep themselves therein, or to persevere? Let
them never be so audacious as to vex with their
importunate presence the Goodman of the House.

III. We now come to the *vices of the body*,
which put obstacles in the way of the ecclesiastical
state.

We may consider as a sign of non-vocation,
whatever may be the piety of the subject, any considerable deformities which compromise the dignity
of the person, infirmities or mutilations which render the functions of the sacred ministry physically
or morally impossible; or periodical maladies whose

attacks excite fear or disgust. Those whom God
afflicts with these temporal miseries ought to seek
in the exercise of Christian patience and resignation
those merits which others find in a holy vocation.
In refusing to them the natural qualities necessary
for the exercise of the priesthood, God clearly
shows that He does not call them to that holy
state.

As to the extrinsic signs of non-vocation, over
and above those I have pointed out, it is meet to
mention the sacred duty which nature imposes upon
a son—and, in speaking of the religious state, upon
a daughter also—of sustaining their parents in
distress, and of paying back to them the cares
they have received from them in their infancy.
This is a rare case, especially in classes in easy
circumstances; but, when it really does present
itself, it involves a real obligation. The Church,
which grants great and numerous privileges to
the religious state, has ordered, by a special law,
children who are not definitely engaged therein
to quit the cloister and re-enter the world, in
order to acquit themselves of these family duties.
This duty sometimes only lasts a short time; still
it is in many circumstances an obstacle to an
immediate vocation or at least to its execution.

I also call the canonical *irregularities* determined by the laws of the Church an extrinsic
sign of non-vocation. By irregularity we mean a
canonical impediment by which we are forbidden
either to enter the ecclesiastical state, or else to
receive an order superior to that which we have

already received, or to exercise the functions of the order with which we are invested.

The irregularities of the first kind, *i.e.*, those which prevent entry into the ecclesiastical state, are the only ones to be taken into account when deliberating on the choice of a state of life. Some are only temporary, *e.g.*, under age ; others suppose some grave sin, others loss of good name. It belongs to the director, rather than to him who is deliberating, to know and interpret them all. It will suffice for us to have recalled them. Still, we may add that notorious scandals, loss of honour, or the brand of infamy incurred by a judicial sentence, as well as enormous and public sins, oppose a manifest obstacle to entering the ecclesiastical state.

Lastly, those who meet with difficulties of fortune, or a deliberate and constant opposition on the part of their superiors, must be persuaded that God does not call them to this state.

Such is what I desired to say concerning the signs of non-vocation to the priesthood.

CHAPTER IX.

Of the Enormity of the Sin of those who enter the Priestly State without being called of God.

We scarcely now-a-days meet any longer with young men, or families, who, audaciously braving both human and Divine laws, cry out, without shame

or modesty, "Let us strive to possess the sanctuary
of the Lord for an inheritance," and who possess
themselves, if they can, of the ecclesiastical functions as of their own goods. Attempts of this kind
were witnessed when the riches of the Church
tempted the cupidity of the men of the world, and
in ages when might easily prevailed against right.
These deplorable excesses belong not to our century.
Yet other dangers surround the entrance of the
sanctuary.

Families are to be met with who, being but
slightly blessed with the gifts of fortune, and burdened with a great number of children, desire, seek
after, and foster a vocation to the ecclesiastical state
as a means of suitably establishing a young man
who would with difficulty carve a career out for
himself in the world, or even in order to satisfy a
piety in other respects sincere. It is an honour, a
guarantee of peace and good example for all the
members of the family, to possess under the roof of
the paternal home a minister of God, called by the
name of son or brother. Parents moved by these
thoughts, whether pious or worldly, exercise an
influence on their child's will, represent to him the
advantages of the priesthood, the inconveniences
and difficulties of another career, and so prepare
him insensibly for the ecclesiastical state.

If God by His inward graces answers these invitations that come from without, well and good.
But if He does not throw open the sanctuary to
these children, such tendencies and efforts become a
perfidious snare, a real danger.

It may also happen that a young man, seeing but a poor future in the world, is carried by purely temporal motives towards the career of the priesthood, and does violence to himself in order to appear worthy of it. He hides his defects, dissembles his repugnance, makes no advance in virtue: he has in view only an honourable position and a certain ease of life. Here again is a dangerous snare, a great peril.

We will shortly prove to persons exposed to yield to temptations of this sort how guilty they would be, and how unhappy, if they were to succumb.

To usurp the priesthood without vocation is to do a great injury to God, a great wrong to the Church, and to prepare for oneself eternal misery.

To begin with, it is doing a great injury to God. We have already proved that at all times God has reserved to Himself the choice of his priests as a right of His sovereignty and a mark of His empire over souls. Under the law of nature and under the written law He only admitted to the service of His altar those priests whom He had Himself marked out and chosen. He has reserved to Himself the same right under the law of grace, beneath which we live. More than this, He has foretold by the mouth of Isaias that He determines to exercise this right of Himself. Foreseeing the conversion of the pagan peoples and their entry into the kingdom of the Messias, He says, " I will take of them," *i.e.*, " the nations to be priests and Levites."* Our Heavenly Master proclaimed this sovereign right

* Is. lxvi. 21.

during His mortal life, not only by His example in choosing His Apostles and consecrating them Himself, but also by His speech. "I am the door," He saith to His disciples; "all others as many as have come in" by other ways "are thieves and robbers." * In another place He brands as "wolves in sheeps' clothing" the pastors who thrust themselves into the management of the flock without being sent by the Master.† As soon as He turns His attention to the future of His people and the election of His ministers, He appears preoccupied with this sovereign right which He has reserved to Himself, and which He has willed to exercise in all times.

This right has never been violated with impunity in the past, nor will it ever be so in aftertime. Under the Old Law God pronounced a terrible anathema against the usurpers of the priesthood. Speaking to Moses He said: "Thou shalt appoint Aaron and his sons over the service of the priesthood. The stranger that approacheth to minister shall be put to death."‡ This threat was executed to the letter, even in the lifetime of Moses. Who has not read with fear the punishment suffered by Core, Dathan and Abiron, who were swallowed up by the yawning earth into hell, as Holy Writ says, with their families and their goods, for having attempted to burn incense that God would not accept from their hands?§ Who does not remember the fate of Saul, after his offering the

* John x. 7—9.   † Matt. vii. 15.   ‡ Numb. iii. 10.
§ Numb. xvi. 30—33.

sacrifices that the priests alone had the right to
offer? He was rejected, he and his family, from
the face of the Lord, and deprived for ever of the
House of Israel.* Oza, for having put his hand
upon the Ark of the Covenant, notwithstanding
God's prohibition, for fear lest it should fall, was
striken instantaneously with death by an unseen
hand.† Are not these examples very significant?
Do they not prove that usurpation of the priesthood or of priestly functions is punished with spiritual death under the New Law, as it was with bodily
death under the old? Conjectures are quite superfluous: our Saviour has clearly expressed Himself
on the subject. He has depicted the usurpers of
the new priesthood in the most lively colours when
He represented them to us as wolves in sheeps'
clothing; as thieves and assassins, who enter into
the good man's house elsewhere than by the door.
What, according to the Gospel, do devouring
wolves, assassins and thieves deserve, if not death?
But what completely developes His thoughts on
the subject is the place He reserves for them at
the last doom. Then these false prophets, who
have thrust themselves into the priesthood uncalled, will cast about for excuses; they will say
to the Sovereign Judge: "Lord, Lord, have we
not prophesied in Thy name and cast out devils in
Thy name?" And the Sovereign Judge will
answer them: "I never knew you; depart from
me you that work iniquity."‡ In other words:

* 1 Kings xiii. 14.   † 2 Kings vi. 6, 7.
‡ Matt. vii. 15, 22, 23.

Ye shall never have any part in my kingdom; no share remains for you but the lot of the damned.

It is a very noteworthy thing, and well calculated to check those rash souls who are tempted to usurp the priesthood without vocation, to observe the manner in which our Heavenly Master describes this terrible scene of the last doom. In the mouth of the Sovereign Judge He only puts two principal reproaches by way of example, viz., usurpation of the sacred ministry, which is contrary to Divine charity or the love of God; and hardness to the poor, which is contrary to the love of our neighbour—as though to make us understand that there are no crimes which lead more infallibly to everlasting punishment.

Thus usurpation of the priesthood under the New Law, as under the Old, has for its final chastisement the punishment of death. This terrible chastisement is inflicted for two reasons: firstly, because this usurpation constitutes, as we have just seen, an outrageous violation of the sovereign rights which God has reserved to Himself in the government and administration of His people; next, because this usurpation causes disturbance in the order of His Providence, as we will now explain:—

Just as in the physical order God confers part of His benefits upon us by the intermediation of secondary causes, by the action of creatures obeying His laws and communicating to us His gifts, so in the order of grace God communicates His benefits to us by the intermediation of the Church—

a supernatural world, a world of grace, if I may
so speak, the providential source of sanctification
placed between God and ourselves, as a link, as a
channel, as a Divine instrument, which has its
proper action determined by Providence, willed
by God, but left to herself in such manner that
our Saviour, after having instituted her by an
action of His merciful and all-powerful arm,
operates no more miracles to determine her effects,
but lets her act according to ordinary laws, established once for all. Now this Church, which is
in the order of grace a supernatural nature acting
of herself, is founded and built upon the priesthood. It is by the hierarchy of her ministers
that she acts, governs, directs and sanctifies.
Bishops and priests are then, in the plans of
Divine Providence, the dispensers of sacred things,
the pastors of souls, the ministers of sanctification,
the ordinary instruments of Divine goodness. On
their action definitely depends all the evil that the
Church endeavours to prevent, and all the good that
she strives to effect in the world. Thus the Providential action of the Divine goodness upon souls
ransomed by the blood of Jesus Christ is finally
summed up in the activity, more or less energetic,
holy, wise, or constant, of the Catholic priesthood.

This being premised, we see at once how the usurpation of the priesthood disturbs the order of Divine
Providence. To usurp the priesthood is to lay a
hand, and that a profane one, upon the basis of that
sacred building whose only Architect is our Lord
Jesus Christ; to add a profane stone to the sacred

foundation laid by the Hand of the Most High; to undertake, with mere human strength, labours which can only be accomplished by the help of Divine strength; to base upon nature a work that has its basis essentially upon grace; to attribute to man a mission that can only come from God. As water, infected in its source, poisons all the river-banks by which it flows, so an ecclesiastic infected, if I may so say, with a purely human vocation, can only seduce, ruin, damn the souls confided to him, and introduce a deplorable confusion in the midst of the flock, to which he ought to be the providential instrument of grace and sanctification.

Is it, then, so difficult to conceive the enormity of this crime, and to appreciate the just rigour with which God punishes it?

This crime, again, does injury to our holy mother the Church, and causes her deplorable damages. The anathemas which her Divine Master hath uttered in the Gospel against usurpation of the ecclesiastical state the Church has inserted in her canons and made the basis of her discipline. *She*, too, drives away the wolves that ravage her flock and trouble her fold; *she*, too, condemns the thieves who come to carry off her treasures, that is, the souls of her children. Thus, by usurping the priesthood in spite of her laws, a wound is inflicted both in her rights and in her affections, and the gravest injury is done to her. Moreover, she is deceived in a very important matter and in her dearest interests. It is less as queen than as mother that the Church provides for the succession of the priest-

hood and the recruiting of her ministers. This
conclusion is naturally drawn from the rite of
ordination, in which the archdeacon, as he presents
to the bishop the subjects to be ordained, says to
him : "Our holy mother the Church begs of you
that you would ordain these subdeacons to the
charge of the deaconate. . . . Our holy mother
the Church begs of you that you would ordain
these deacons to the charge of the priesthood."
And the bishop asking him, who at this solemn
juncture is the spokesman of the Church, says :
"Knowest thou them to be worthy?" And the
archdeacon answers: "As far as human frailty
allows me to know, I believe and testify that they
are worthy of the charge of this office." And the
bishop answers: "God be thanked!"* This solemn
scene indicates both the confidence which the
Church puts in the fitness and faithfulness of the
subjects she presents for ordination, and the hopes
that she founds upon them. What a cruel deception, what a subject of confusion for her, when
the subjects thus presented are not really worthy ;
when they have positively and knowingly deceived
their mother; when they have put on her lips,
by their trickery and hypocrisy, an attestation
which in God's eyes is a lie! Fancy a Christian
who in good sooth would dare to render himself
guilty of such a crime! He would insult his
spiritual mother by deceiving her in the exercise of her motherly duties, so as to make her

* Pontificale Romanum : de Ordin : Diaconi, Presbyteri.

serve as the instrument of malice and hypocrisy, and that in the very midst of the sacred ordination!

Again, is not this deception the first link of a long chain of deceptions still more cruel to her mother's heart? Who can enumerate all the ravages that a priest, who has entered the ecclesiastical state without vocation, causes in the midst of the fold of the Good Shepherd? He is a wolf, tearing, slaughtering, devouring; he is a torrent, undermining, overturning, sweeping away; a fire, kindling, devouring, consuming; a demon, seducing, misleading, damning! There is no human speech with terms strong enough to express the damage caused to God's people by an unworthy minister who has usurped the priesthood, in despite of the laws of God and of the Church, and who becomes an instrument of death when he ought to be a source of life.

How could the Church fail to bemoan so bitter a deception! She would behold her spiritual hierarchy dishonoured in one of its members; the spiritual beauty of her body sullied and disfigured in one of her chiefs; the sacred ministry interrupted and poisoned by one of her ministers; the souls of her children lost by coming upon a stone of stumbling, in the very place where they should have found nothing but holiness and edification! And should she not moan, should she not shed tears over this unworthy minister as bitter as those with which Jeremias watered the scattered stones of the sanctuary of Sion? Ah! he who believes the Church to be insensible to such great

woes knows her not! But nobody can deceive
himself on this point; and as soon as he has comprehended the immensity of her grief in such a
case, how can he so far forget it as to become a
cause of it to her?

Nor is this all. He who usurps the priesthood
without vocation is also paving the way for his
own misery. We may compare him to the Apostles,
St. John and St. James, at the time when they
still followed the inspirations of human ambition.
One day their mother approached our Saviour and
said: "Say that these my two sons may sit, the
one on Thy right hand, and the other on Thy left,
in Thy kingdom." And Jesus, answering, said:
"You know not what you ask."* We should
make the same reply, or rather, a secret voice
would make it, to young men who should dare to
penetrate into the sanctuary without being called
of God: "You know not what you ask!"

Doubtless, the priesthood is a sublime dignity,
a state of holiness which lifts up man to the rank
of the angels, a profession which associates him in
the functions of the sacred hosts, a ministry which
puts him in habitual communication with God
Himself. But, on the other hand, the priesthood
is a dreadful burden; it imposes enormous duties,
the gravest obligations and most weighty charges.
When God calls one of His servants to this holy
state, all difficulties disappear through the operation
of grace, which proportions the strength of the soul

* Matt. xx. 21, 22.

to the extent of its duties, and upholds human weakness by Divine help.

But imagine a man who, abandoned to his natural strength, undertakes to carry this burden alone, unaided, unhelped! If ever he succeed in taking it up on his shoulders, he will be infallibly crushed by it.

The spectacle of an unhappy young man engaged, in spite of God, in the bonds of the priesthood, would be enough, if it were fully comprehended, to turn away for ever those who aspire thereto without vocation. Hardly are his destinies fixed for ever, when the unhappy man takes his hand off the plough; he looks behind him, and sighs after a liberty henceforward impossible. Wearisomeness attacks him hourly; bitter regrets torment him without respite; passions without bridle, as well as without food, like so many vultures, eat his heart and cause him perpetual torments. If he turn his gaze to the past, he sees nothing therein but his faults, his weaknesses, his falsehoods, his hypocrisy, or his blind obstinacy. If he consider the present, he beholds himself on an impracticable road, on a path that has no turning; he recognizes that he is burdened with functions, which are subjects of dread to men and angels, and feels himself unable to fulfil them. If he contemplate the future, he discovers nothing but awful anathemas launched by God's justice against the usurpers of the priesthood. He trembles, he shudders at the spectacle. For can we conceive a more dreadful situation? Is there on earth a man more unfortunate? And for

the sake of a few honours, of a handful of gold, a
man would hurl himself into this abyss! Why,
even if faith were to fail, surely sound reason would
turn him away from it.

No motive can prevail over the considerations
just detailed. Yet men have found pretexts to
colour or excuse the usurpation of ecclesiastical
functions. Isaias, it is said, presented himself to
the Lord and said: "Lo! here am I, send me." *
Yes, but do people reflect that Isaias was inspired?
—that he was offering himself for a temporary
mission and not to enter into a permanent state?
Above all, that he was *offering* himself to God, but
not *thrusting* himself upon Him; and that, far
from usurping the mission in spite of the decrees
of Providence, he was begging for it!

All the faithful are, without doubt, free to offer
themselves to God, and to the Church, provided
that they withdraw when they are not accepted.

But if you seek examples of this sort among the
saints of the Old Testament, you will certainly find
many of them who have accepted with fear and
trembling the Divine mission that Heaven imposed
upon them. Moses conjured God to send to His
people, then in bondage to Egypt, some other
deliverer than himself. "Send," said he, "whom
Thou wilt send;" † send the man according to Thy
own heart, but deliver me from this difficult undertaking. "Ah! ah! ah!" cried out the Prophet
Jeremias before the Lord, "I cannot speak;" ‡

---

* Is. vi. 8.   † Ex. iv. 13.   ‡ Jer. i. 6.

how am I to announce Thy word? Jonas, terrified
by the heavenly mission, endeavoured to withdraw
himself from it by flight.* Here, then, are sentiments of self-distrust and fear of God suitable to
all the faithful who positively doubt of the reality
of their vocation to the ecclesiastical state. They
who are animated by them, and who submit themselves to God's will, will never be exposed to a
guilty and fatal usurpation.

But the Apostle says : "If a man desireth the office
of a bishop, he desireth a good work."† Therefore
he does not blame aspiring to Holy Orders.

The Apostle speaks of the aspiration, the desire
which souls called of God feel to share, not in the
honours and temporal advantages of the priesthood,
but in its charges and dangers. I speak of the
episcopate, such as it was in the early ages; yet
we can at the same time understand these words of
the episcopate in all ages, provided that we are
mindful of the qualities which the Apostle exacts
from those who are invested with it. At the time
when St. Paul wrote, the episcopate and the priesthood were the road to martyrdom; nowadays, as
then, they conduce to the welfare of souls and the
glory of God. To desire these things is a "good
work," an act agreeable to God; such is what the
Apostle wished to express. Those who arm themselves with these words in order to cover a sacrilegious usurpation, evidently do not understand them.

But, you reply, the religious state is free; every-

* Jonas i. 3.   † 1 Tim. iii. 1.

body may enter it, provided they are disposed to
fulfil its duties. Our Saviour says to all the faithful, " If thou wilt be perfect, go, sell what thou
hast and give to the poor ; and come, follow me."*
Now, the priesthood is attached, so to speak, to the
religious state ; therefore the priesthood is *im-
plicitly* offered to all the faithful, therefore it is
free for each one to accept it, and ever to seek
after it.

This is not a legitimate conclusion. Although
the Church grants the priesthood a little more
easily to religious than to secular clerics, she has
never considered ordination as a natural or necessary consequence of the religious profession. If
vocation to the religious state has some analogy,
and, if you like, a certain affinity to vocation to
the priestly state, still, in many respects, these vocations differ, and are not connected. Many of the
faithful, called to the religious state by the voice of
Heaven, have no vocation for the priesthood.
Hence the supposed connection does not exist. A
religious, no less than a secular cleric, apart from
holy obedience, which directs him in this as in all
other things, must before receiving Holy Orders
examine his strength and his dispositions, and see
whether he can finish the tower which he proposes
to build.* In other words, whether he be truly
called of God to the priesthood, and if, consequently,
he can persevere in the fulfilment of the duties
which this dignity imposes.

Matt. xix. 21.   Luke xiv. 28, seq.

But there is a lack of priests. Many flocks are wandering for want of pastors. We desire to consecrate ourselves to the welfare of souls.

This is a specious pretext. But, first of all, remember that it belongs not to you, but it is God's business to recruit the ranks of His hosts. He is little troubled at the fewness of His soldiers; very often He grants the victory to a mere handful of combatants. If it be necessary to refer to the history of God's people, we shall see that Gedeon, with three hundred and eighteen soldiers, defeated immense multitudes; that Samson by himself routed armies. In cases of need, angels fight side by side with God's ministers. A single angel in one night exterminated the army of Sennacherib. What God considers and esteems above all in His ministers is the vocation of Heaven, the Divine mission. We read in the history of the Machabees that certain of God's priests wished to distinguish themselves by making war on the foes, but they underwent a bloody defeat. And why? Because "they were not of the seed of those men," says the Holy Spirit, "by whom salvation was brought to Israel."* Nowadays, especially, nothing can replace the Divine vocation in God's priests, and the Church would rather count fewer ministers than have those whom God has not called. Innocent III., that great Pope whose decrees are law in the Church, says in formal terms, in the acts of the Fourth Lateran Council, "It is better, especially

* 1 Mac. v. 62.

in ordaining priests, to have a few good, than many evil ministers ; for, if the blind lead the blind, they both fall into the pit."*

O Lord! Thou who holdest in Thy hands the hearts of men, never permit young Christians to engage themselves in Holy Orders in despite of Thee. Thou didst expel by the ministry of an angel the impious Heliodorus, the audacious minister of a sacreligious king, from the Temple of Jerusalem, whose treasures he wished to plunder. Thou didst Thyself drive from that temple those who bought and sold victims therein. Do not suffer, we conjure Thee, that, in defiance of Thy laws and Thy glory, unworthy children should penetrate into Thy sanctuary in order to make a traffic of the salvation of souls and of Thy sacred mysteries. Close the doors against the hirelings who make the kingdom of God consist in eating and drinking; and only admit these men according to Thine own heart, called like Aaron to the priesthood, and prepared for this dignity by the Holy Spirit. Then will Christian virtues flourish amidst Thy people, and Thy Church shall live in happiness and in joy.

* Lateran Council, A.D. 1215. Canon xxvii. in *Herduin*, vol. vii., col. 42.

CHAPTER X.

Of the Motives and Obligation to follow Divine Vocation to the Ecclesiastical State.

IF there are to be met with young men who try to usurp the priesthood without vocation, there are unhappily others who resist God's voice and refuse the burthen which Heaven wishes to lay upon them. The Church suffers no less from the resistance of pusillanimous hearts than from the rash haste of presumptuous souls. St. John Chrysostom, after weighing in the balance of the sanctuary the wrongs that both do to Divine Providence, assures us that it is probably more dangerous to reject a call to the ecclesiastical state which comes from Heaven than to enter that state without a vocation. This opinion it is easy to justify: for he who usurps the priesthood without vocation, thrusts himself into functions that are not intrusted to him and occupies himself in a ministry which, to say the least, is useless ; but he who refuses the priesthood when God calls him thereto, abandons functions that are destined for him, and leaves a gap in the ranks of the sacred armies. By going away from the fold over which God wishes him to watch, he leaves open one of those entrances by which the wolves will probably make their way to the flock, in order to scatter and devour it. On the one hand there is pride and temerity ; on the other weakness and ingratitude, besides a disobedience which in some cases may reach to a very high degree of gravity.

But, before developing motives of fear, I will detail motives of hope and of love. Although I have already explained. in a few lines the honour and happiness attached to the ecclesiastical vocation, I will here show a little more at large the great value that faith makes us set upon this vocation. I will also recall, as briefly as possible, the dignity, the powers, the holiness, the consolations and the rewards of the priestly state. After having made these motives of obedience to God clearly understood, I will point out, in a few words, how dangerous it is to salvation to resist God's will on this point.

I. We will speak, firstly, of the *dignity* of the priestly state.

The Holy Fathers compare this dignity to that of kings and angels, and put it above both. And, indeed, when we consider the origin, the end, the duration of temporal sovereignty and of the priesthood, we shall easily see that the latter far excels in these respects.

Royalty is an earthly dignity: it has its source in the temporal wants of peoples, is founded on human right, and depends to a great extent on the will of man. The priesthood has a much more noble and independent origin. It emanates from the Divine will, it is founded on the very basis of religion, *i.e.*, on the foundations of the Catholic Church, and it flows from the priesthood of Jesus Christ, the High Priest, according to the order of Melchisedech.

Royalty has for its immediate end the procuring of the temporal well-being of the people, the preserving of social order, the maintenance of individual rights and public security. This is an honourable task, without doubt, but it is less noble than that of the priesthood, which has for its end the procuring of the spiritual well-being of men, the guardianship of their eternal interests, the promulgation and execution of God's laws, and the preparation of everyone, by the exercise of its function, for happiness without end.

Kings, when they die, lose their dignity, and henceforward are like the lowest of their subjects. The priest preserves his priestly character and his dignity for all eternity, for he is " a priest for ever." The death of kings is a sadder event than the death of subjects, because it involves greater and more sensible losses. But the death of a priest adds a new lustre to his dignity by transferring it from earth to heaven.

And this dignity, moreover, surpasses in some respects that of the angels. The angels, indeed, are superior to man by their *nature*, but they are not superior to the priest in their *functions*. The Holy Spirit tells us that angels " are sent to minister for them who shall receive the inheritance of salvation."* Priests lead souls into the grace of salvation, maintain them therein, bring them back thither, and finally introduce them into heaven. In order to save souls, the angels keep an anxious and continual watch over the faithful, and remove from

* Heb. i. 14.

their feet the snares of the evil one. And for the same end priests work a host of wonders by the supernatural power that is given them.

I say *wonders*, because the priest never exercises his priestly power without working a miracle in the order of grace. Whether he absolve repentant sinners, restoring to them their right to Paradise, or call down on to our altars the thrice-holy God, he appears to our eyes a veritable *Thaumaturgus*. Whenever it falls to the holy angels to work miracles in favour of the faithful, it is almost always in the temporal order that they are accomplished. Witness the Angel Raphael healing Tobias, and the avenging angel who exterminated the army of Sennacherib. The priest, on the contrary, exercises his awful power in the supernatural order, and for the healing of souls much more than for the healing of bodies.

II. But what raises priests above all the other ministers of the Divine will, and, we may say, in a sense, above all creatures, is the awful *power* with which they are invested. The priesthood stamps the soul of the priest with a spiritual and ineffaceable character, and this character is the principle of a power, the most astonishing, the most marvellous that can be imagined, that of offering to God the Father the sacrifice of the Spotless Lamb for the expiation of sin and the salvation of the world. Who can reflect on this prodigious power without trembling, and blessing in the fulness of his heart the Divine goodness for having deigned to clothe our miserable humanity with so much strength, so much authority and so much power?   Must we not cry out at this point: O God, All-powerful, how can it be that Thou, the maker of heaven and earth, the Sovereign Master of all things, who balancest the world on the point of Thy finger, who commandest the whole universe, that Thou dost deign to humble Thyself, so as to obey the voice of one of the children of men, to become incarnate in some sort in a new fashion in his feeble hand?   When the orb of day stopped at the voice of Josue the whole of nature was amazed that God, its Author, could obey one of His servants.   What, then, must the angels and the elect think at seeing the God of majesty, the God of all greatness and glory, come down from His throne at the voice of His minister, and, forgetting the canticles of the choirs of heaven, hide Himself in silence beneath the Eucharistic veils, in order to receive there the homage of men and to nourish souls with His sacred Flesh! O marvellous effect of the priestly ministry! The Lord comes not down upon our altars surrounded with glory, as He appeared on Sinai and Thabor; He appears not as a judge, such as He will show Himself at the last day, stern and terrible: He does not even fashion Himself in His humanity, as he was seen in Bethlehem and on the plains of Judea: but He comes in the state of the Victim, humble and hidden, to renew by His adorable presence the Bloody Sacrifice that He offered on Calvary. At the very moment when the priest pronounces the sacramental words, what a spectacle is offered to the eyes of faith! This human voice penetrates even to the heavens : it moves the hierarchy of the angels, it rouses the choirs of the blessed, and the inhabitants of the heavenly Jerusalem, veiling their faces with their wings, come down in one body with the Man-God, in order to adore and serve Him. Ranged around the altar, where the spotless Victim smokes for our salvation, they cover their faces, they cast themselves down in spirit, and there address to Him their supplications in man's behalf. Then, too, the sacred chaunts echo under the vaults of the temple, the people, prostrate, strike their breasts and implore the mercy of God the Saviour. But, whilst all bend down and prostrate around the altar, the priest alone stands up in the midst of this venerable assembly : he lifts towards heaven the Sacred Victim and thus offers It to God the Father, who accepts It from his hands for the reconciliation of the world.

What power and grandeur do we not perceive here in the priesthood! What a precious dignity in the eyes of faith! And, consequently, what happiness to be associated therein by virtue of a decree of the Divine will!

The power which the priest exercises over the real Body of our Lord Jesus Christ on earth, to sanctify souls in His name whilst sanctifying himself—what a happy portion for a true child of the Church!

III. To the supernatural dignity and power of the priesthood we must add its astonishing holiness.

All in this state is holy, all therein is a source of holiness. It is holy in its source, which is the eternal priesthood of Jesus Christ, the High Priest

according to the order of Melchisedech and Sovereign
Pontiff of all the elect. The priests of the Church
hold in this world the place of our Lord Himself,
who baptizes, absolves, consecrates and blesses by
their hands. In their sacred ministry they are, so
to speak, identified with our Divine Saviour, and
by this title they share, without the least doubt, in
His ineffable sanctity.

The priesthood is holy in its consecration. It is
conferred by the sacrament of Order which the
Eastern Churches call a "mystery," because it
contains a sublime and hidden operation of the
hand of God, impressing on the priest's soul a
Divine character, a new resemblance with God, the
Sanctifier of souls. The sacrament of Order consecrates to God him who receives it, and, whilst
conferring on him a supernatural power, it ensures to
him the graces necessary for exercising it worthily.
It is to priests especially that God says : "Be ye
holy, because I, the Lord your God, am holy."*

The priesthood is holy in its aim. It has been
instituted to sanctify God's people by the application of the merits of our Lord Jesus Christ. Our
Lord poured out His blood in order that His
Church might be holy and without spot ; He instituted the priesthood of the New Covenant in
order to apply the price of this Divine Blood to
the faithful, and to render them truly holy. God
wills that we all be holy, as the Apostle expressly
teaches.†

The priesthood is holy in its functions. With

* Levit. xix. 2.   † 1 Thess. iv. 3.

what is the priest of God occupied?   He adores
God and praises Him in the name of His people,
as an earthly mediator between the King of Heaven
and His exiled family in this world.   It is he who
admits into Holy Church young children, by conferring Baptism upon them; it is he who absolves
sinners, remitting their sins; it is he who feeds the
faithful with the Bread of Life at the Sacred Table;
it is he who blesses marriage ; it is he who fortifies
and consoles the dying; it is he who sanctifies the
tomb of the dead.   To spread the light of faith in
souls, to plant Christian virtues in the heart, and
to root out vices ; to bring back strayed sheep to the
fold ; to preserve the lambs from the wolves' fangs ;
to feed, heal, and keep his flock ; to act now as a
father, now as a physician, now as a judge; to
reconcile earth to heaven; to sanctify the earth,
in order that it may become worthy of heaven ; to
offer to God the prayers and merits of the faithful ;
to ask of God His most abundant graces for His
children : such are the principal functions of the
priest.   The priesthood is thus holy by means of
the sanctification it brings upon all the faithful.
If it were to disappear from the Church, all the
well-springs of holiness would be at once dried up
and the road to heaven closed for ever.

The priesthood is also holy by reason of the
holiness it brings to him who is invested with it.
The priest of the New Covenant is truly sanctified
in his whole person in virtue of his holy state.   By
the sacrament of Order he receives, in addition to
an increase of sanctifying grace, a Divine stamp, a

supernatural fitness to exercise the functions of the priesthood of Jesus Christ. His body also is sanctified in divers manners. His hands are consecrated by the sacred unction, and receive the power of blessing, sanctifying and consecrating. His lips are destined to pronounce the sacramental words that come forth from the mouth of our Divine Saviour—words which work miracles in the order of grace, and, by their effects, penetrate, as we have already remarked, heaven and hell. His tongue is daily stained with the Precious Blood of the Immaculate Lamb. His eyes are fixed on the Sacred Victim, and incessantly peruse the Sacred Books, in order to draw thence the word of God, so as to announce His oracles to the Church. When he preaches this word of God, when he meditates upon it, in order to make it known to his flock, what a light then bursts forth in his mind, what a sweet warmth spreads in his heart! And it is the same with all his functions.

Innumerable outward means also help him to attain to a high degree of holiness. The laws of the Church, the canons of councils, the solicitude of the superior pastors, the example of his comrades who accompany him, or follow him, or perhaps even precede him in the practice of priestly virtues ; even the counsels and advice that are asked of him with simplicity and confidence, are so many stimulants which urge him on in the path of priestly perfection, so many efficacious means to preserve him from sin, and to make him reach a high degree of holiness.

The priesthood is thus eminently holy, and for

this reason infinitely worthy of exciting the pious
ambition of a soul that sincerely loves our Lord.

IV. What shall I say next of the consolations
of the priest in his sacred ministry? They are
innumerable, they are immense; they are sufficient to render sweet and light all the trials and
tribulations of this life.

To begin with: the priest enjoys the sweetest of
consolations in those which he procures in such
number for the souls entrusted to him. The Holy
Spirit, whom our Lord calls the Comforter, is given
to him, together with the priesthood, in order that
he himself may be the comforter of his brethren,
and that the unction of his word may bring
patience, resignation and peace into all hearts.
As a pastor and a father he enjoys the confidence
and love of his family, his flock. To him the unfortunate and the afflicted have recourse; with him
they find peace, joy and happiness. Is a family
stricken in one of its members, is a Christian at the
point of death, does Providence permit a trial to afflict
any one, the priest is the first who runs up to soften
the blow that is dealt or threatened. This ministry
of consolation has evidently its charms; it is impossible for a priest to exercise it without drawing thence
pure joy and abundant consolations for himself.

I have spoken of the outward ministry; but how
can I forget what I may call the inward ministry
of the priest—I mean that life recollected in, and
all devoted to, God?—that ardent desire of priestly
perfection?—those constant aspirations to sanctity?—that unshaken faithfulness to all the duties

of the priesthood?—that continual communication with Heaven, which constitute at bottom the priest's life and are so many channels of heavenly grace? It is impossible for a minister of God attached to his duties not to receive from God abundant consolations, and especially that constancy and strength of soul which enable him to surmount and despise all miseries and all difficulties. To a priest according to God's own heart the injuries of impious men, the calumnies of false brethren, the contempt of the wicked, the attacks of unbelievers, the assaults of sickness, bodily fatigues, the persecutor's sword—all that is heavy, bitter or insupportable to nature, is, as it were, absorbed by inward consolations, and leaves in the soul no print of sorrow. Voluntarily exiled in the midst of barbarous nations, overwhelmed with labours, worn out with fatigue, threatened on all sides, St. Francis Xavier, the *Thaumaturgus* of modern times, received such abundant consolations from Heaven that he was heard even in his sleep to cry out: "Too much, O Lord, too much!" He could not contain this cry of gratitude and love that was bursting from his heart; his lips uttered it almost unknown to him, because it came out from the depths of his heart. Such was also the lot of St. Paul, who wrote to his terrified disciples: " I exceedingly abound with joy in all our tribulations."*

V. Lastly, the *reward* of priests is immense. God will restore to each one according to his merits. Now nobody has more means or opportunities of

* 2 Cor. vii. 4.

increasing the store of his merits than the priest, for he is incessantly busied in meritorious action. If martyrdom and virginity merit from Heaven a special crown, we must believe that the priesthood will have its own also. The pastors of souls, who preside here below in the gatherings of the faithful, will also preside in heaven in the choirs of the elect; and, as pre-eminence in the heavenly Jerusalem is the measure of glory and happiness, the priests of God, if they have answered to their holy vocation, will be happier therein than the rest of the faithful.

Such, in a few pages, is a summary of the motives of love and hope which ought to determine pusillanimous hearts to follow the vocation which God offers them or imposes upon them. We will now say a few words on the motives of fear.

Sacred history tells us that God does not suffer resistance to the plans of His mercy to go unpunished. I will cite two striking examples of the misfortunes to which we are exposed in rejecting the offers of His goodness.

The Prophet Jonas, having disobeyed the order of God, either through fear or through pusillanimity, compromised the lives of all those who were sailing with him. This is a striking image of the misfortunes to which we expose others by rejecting the call of Heaven. He was only able to put aside the danger which threatened the ship by sacrificing himself, throwing himself into God's arms, in order to accomplish, if Providence still wished it, the mission he had refused. If the prophet, unfaithful in the first instance, had not

accepted the vocation which God imposed upon
him, it is probable that he would have perished
with all on board.

We have another no less striking example of
the manner in which God abandons the faithful
who draw back, when He calls them to a perfect
life, in the young man of the Gospel. This young
man one day came to our Divine Master and
said : "Good Master, what good shall I do that
I may have life everlasting ? " Jesus said to him :
" If thou wilt enter into life keep the commandments." The young man replied : " All these have
I kept from my youth, what is yet wanting to
me ? " Jesus said to him : " If thou wilt be perfect, go sell what thou hast and give to the poor,
and thou shalt have treasure in heaven : and come,
follow me." And when the young man had heard
this word, he went away sad—for he had great
possessions. Then Jesus said to His disciples :
" Amen, I say to you, that a rich man shall hardly
enter into the kingdom of heaven."* Every word
of this history contains a lesson. The young man
presents himself to our Saviour, having been in
the most favourable dispositions to follow Him from
his infancy : he has observed all the commandments and feels the desire of doing more for God.
The Divine Master receives him with goodness,
and evinces His · tender affection for him. He
points out to him he way of the perfect life open
before him, and invites him to enter it. But
the young man lacks courage to part from his

* Mat. xix. 16 seq.

goods, and goes away full of sadness, unable to
make up his mind to follow the advice he had
asked. Strictly, we might have believed that a
young man, by rejecting the vocation of God and
refusing to embrace the perfect life, had not compromised his salvation. But our Saviour draws a
very different conclusion. How difficult, says He,
for rich men to enter the kingdom of heaven.
As though He would say: Those who, like this
unhappy man, reject the pressing invitation of
Heaven for riches' sake, or who renounce a certain
vocation through attachment to this world, will
never reach the port of salvation. It is thus that
the ancient fathers have understood our Saviour's
words, and thus must we understand it.* What
a terrible lesson for pusillanimous souls! What a
powerful motive to give oneself to God when He
asks it!

When we think of the gravity of such a refusal,
and count the sins it involves, we cannot be
astonished at the terrible consequences which the
Gospel attributes to it. God calls us as would
a counsellor or a friend. Hence such a refusal
involves an act of great temerity, because in resisting we prefer our own lights to God's. God calls
us as Creator and a Sovereign. Hence such a
refusal involves an injustice, because we fail to
consecrate to Him a life and existence of which
He has good right to dispose. God also calls us

* Bourdaloue arrives at the same conclusions in his
Pensées, in which he treats of vocation to the religious
life. Works, vol. xv., p. 122, ed. Besançon, 1823.

as Legislator: to refuse, therefore, involves an act
of disobedience, for it is violating a law, a formal
precept imposed by Him. Lastly, God calls us as
a Father and Benefactor; and thus refusal involves
ingratitude, for it is to recoil before the obligation of giving back to God what we have received
from Him. The ingratitude of such a course is
very sensible. Vocation to the ecclesiastical state
is a sign of predilection on our Lord's part. He
who is called to the priesthood ought to believe
that our Divine Saviour says to him as to Peter:
" Lovest thou me?*" And if he reject this vocation he really answers: " No, Lord, I love Thee
not."

All that you are, all that you possess in the
order of nature, as in the order of grace, comes
to you from God: in inviting you to the priesthood, He asks of you a thousand times less than
He has done for you; and in return for your
offering, or, if you like, for your sacrifice, He
offers you again unnumbered graces, a hundred
means of salvation, which the ordinary faithful
never enjoy in the world. But, in drawing back,
you are unwilling to do anything for Him. It
is the height of ingratitude, it is an egotism that
must wound Him to the heart.

Pretexts, I know, are never wanting, when
sought for to cover one's pusillanimity under these
circumstances; but, believe me, if they sometimes
delude men, they never obtain credit with God;

* John xxi. 16.

and, consequently, furnish no excuse. People will
plead love of parents, attachment to riches, weakness, the burdens of the priesthood. In the presence of a Divine call, all these things are nothing.
Love of parents is, doubtless, very lawful; God
himself enjoins it: but God wills that this love
should be subordinated to that due to Himself.
"He that loveth father or mother more than me,"
He says in His Gospel, "is not worthy of me." *
"Since we must love even our enemies," says St.
Gregory the Great, "how is it true that under
certain circumstances we must hate our neigh-
bours? In this sense," replies the holy doctor,
"that we must love our parents, cherish our neigh-
bours, so long as they aid us in the practice of
good, and that we must leave them and fly from
them as soon as they lead us to evil, or impede us
in doing the good that God requires from us." †
Supposing a Divine vocation to be manifest, St.
Jerome writes to Heliodorus : "Even when a little
grandson clings to your neck: when a tender
mother, with garments rent and hair dishevelled,
shows you the breast that was given you to suck :
even when your father throws himself on the
ground to bar your passage : step over your father's
body, and fly, without shedding a tear, to the
standard of the cross. It is an act of true piety to
be cruel in these circumstances." ‡   St. Fulgentius

* Mat. x. 37.
† St. Gregory the Great, *Homilies*, 37, on the Gospel of
Luke xiv. 26.
‡ St. Jerome, Ep. xiv. 2 to Heliodorus; vol. i., col. 29,
ed. Vallarsi.

entered a monastery and gave himself to God, despite of the tears, groans and supplications of his mother. St. Frances of Chantal stepped over her son's body, who, in order to stop her, had lain down on the threshold of her door. St. Stanislas Kostka left his father's house, despite the refusal and resistance of his father, and gave himself to God, who claimed him. See what the saints have done: see what he must do who wishes to save himself, when he is called like the saints.

Here, again, it is easy to justify the precept of the Gospel at the tribunal of reason. Is it not true, young Christian, that you belong to God before belonging to your parents, and that you belong to Him on more titles than to the authors of your life? Your parents themselves belong to Him, and, by consecrating yourself to Him, they only give back to Him what they have received from His goodness. Remember, then, when God calls you, that, if you have a father on earth, you have another in heaven. The rights of your Heavenly Father have a vast preference over those of your family, which can never claim the right to compromise your eternity. What would it profit them to have given you the life of the body, if a misplaced affection were to cause the death of your soul? Attachment to one's family is, therefore, a natural, lawful and obligatory feeling, but essentially subordinate to the love of God, which, in the last resort, must always prevail over the Christian heart. But what about riches, goods of fortune, and the comforts of life?

Are we, then, made for these things? How long shall we possess them! A few years, a few weeks, perhaps only a few days! And are we to sacrifice our salvation for their sake? Have we forgotten those striking words of our Saviour: " What doth it profit a man if he gain the whole world and suffer the loss of his own soul? Or what exchange shall a man give for his soul?" * Would we have Him repeat for us what He said when the young man in the Gospel went away from Him full of sadness: " How hardly shall they that have riches enter into the kingdom of God!" † He did not apply this word to all rich men, but to those who attach themselves to the goods of earth as to their sovereign happiness and last end: to such as prefer their riches to keeping God's commandments, to the bliss of heaven. Tremble, therefore, if you are resisting the voice of grace for the sake of riches, or through attachment to the goods of earth!

You speak of the comforts of life: but God speaks to you of His afflicted Church, and invites you to labour in His vineyard : He speaks to you of paradise, where a splendid crown is awaiting you. Reflect, then, once for all, on the shortness of this life, whose comforts you seek ; think of the nearness of death, the uncertainty of the goods of fortune, the void they leave in the soul when we cleave to them ; and compare the frail and fleeting advantages which they offer you with the privilege of

* Mat. xvi. 26.   † Mark x. 23.

consecrating yourself at the altar of the true God and meriting an immense glory and endless happiness. When I see a young man, truly called of God, hesitating to follow his vocation, I seem to hear repeated against him the reproach which God addressed to His ungrateful and unfaithful people: " They set at nought the desirable land:" * they have despised my most precious gifts.

But I am weak and frail: how can I, a poor reed, bear a burden that would appear terrible to the very angels? You are weak and frail of yourself, I grant it; but you are powerful in Him who strengthens you, because He calls you to the sublime state of the priesthood. This God of truth hath said that His yoke is sweet and His burden light. And why? Because He has given to each one the helps he needs to fulfil his duties. God tempts no man above his strength, but grants to each the means of carrying the burden He imposed upon His Apostles. When our Lord Jesus Christ called His Apostles to preach the Gospel, were they very strong, very perfect? When He sent them to conquer the world, were they more valiant, more veteran, stronger than you? Had they not their defects and weaknesses? Could they not have objected to their sacred vocation a thousand pretexts more specious than yours? Their ignorance, their rudeness, their toilsome and poor life, their long-standing trade, their nakedness: did they not appear to impede their sublime calling? No; as

* Ps. cv. 24.

soon as our Sàviour spake to them, "they immediately, leaving their nets, followed Him." *
Their Divine Master was then leading an obscure
life, or, rather, had only just left it. He was persecuted, threatened and caluminated by the doctors
of the Synagogue. Nothing stopped His disciples ;
as soon as He had manifested to them God's will,
they followed Him without hesitation, and the
event proved how powerful the grace of vocation
had made them. Notwithstanding their ignorance,
grossness and poverty, they confounded the wise,
converted the most highly organized peoples, and
inspired the most opulent families with a contempt
for riches. Let their example be a lesson to you.
The Apostles followed our Divine Saviour when He
was still despised by men and possessed no other
attraction than that of His grace. Nowadays He
has risen again from the tomb ; He has ascended
in glory to heaven, where He reigns at His Father's
right hand, destined to put all His enemies one
day beneath His feet : and will you hesitate to
follow Him, to obey His voice ? You see that He
has chosen the weak to confound the strong, that
He has sent His disciples as lambs in the midst of
wolves, and that by their ministry He has changed
the wolves into lambs. And are you still afraid,
because of your weakness ? Your fear would have
some foundation if you had to reckon only upon
your own individual strength, but He declares that
He will Himself be your strength and your stay.

* Mat. iv. 20.

If He caused Peter to walk on the water, can He not guard and uphold your footsteps in the path by which He calls you? Count, then, upon Him, whilst mistrusting yourself, and thenceforward fear nought. For as long as He fights with you, the powers of hell will never triumph over your weakness. Be, then, quite convinced that this fear and terror are snares that the devil lays to withdraw you from the sanctuary wherein you can work efficaciously for God's glory and the welfare of souls. Despise his pusillanimous suggestions and throw yourself into your Saviour's arms. As soon as your resolution is taken, the phantoms which darkened and pursued you will vanish like smoke that is scattered before the wind. You will cry out with the Prophet David, "How lovely are Thy tabernacles, O Lord of Hosts!" * "One thing I have asked of the Lord, this will I seek after: that I may dwell in the house of the Lord all the days of my life." † "For better is one day in Thy courts above thousands . . . in the tabernacle of sinners." ‡ Nobody, O Lord, after resisting Thee hath found peace; come, then, into my heart and reign therein for ever, for Thine I am in life and death.

* Ps. lxxxviii. 2. † Ps. xxvi. 4.
‡ Ps. lxxxiii. 11.

CHAPTER XI.

Of the Religious State: Its Origin, Aim, Nature and Properties.

THE religious state is known to all the faithful as a state of sacrifice in which man offers himself up to God in order to please Him, and thus to attain more easily his own salvation. And even simple and unlearned souls, whom God often calls to the religious state by very efficacious and pressing means, have no other idea of it. Still, it is fitting in this place to explain very shortly the origin, aim, nature and properties of the religious state, in order that young people who feel themselves called thereto may be able to embrace it with a full knowledge of the case.

If we consider only the general laws of Christianity, it seems certain that ordinary Christian life in the world is a holy life, a life which leads to holiness. The ordinary means of sanctification are abundantly sufficient for the bulk of the faithful to enable them to sanctify themselves amidst the duties of common life, and thus to arrive at their salvation. The Apostle tells us that our Saviour shed His blood "that He might sanctify His Church "* altogether, and very often he calls the ordinary faithful "saints,"† in order to remind them that they have been sanctified by Baptism,

---

* Eph. v. 26.   † Rom. i. 7 ; 1 Cor. i. 2, etc.

and are obliged to make their way to a greater degree of sanctity by observing God's commandments and practising Christian virtues. In this sense St. Peter calls the faithful " a chosen generation, a kingly priesthood, a holy nation."* Still, over and above the common life, which is sanctified by the keeping of the *precepts*, our Saviour has instituted a more perfect manner of living founded on the observation of the evangelical *counsels*. By evangelical counsels we mean certain practices that our Saviour has recommended to such of His children as aspire to evangelical perfection, but has not imposed upon all the faithful. Three principal counsels are recognized : those of perfect obedience, perfect chastity and perfect poverty. By embracing the perpetual and constant observance of these three counsels, by means of a firm and solemn resolution, or else by taking public vows, the religious state is entered.

Our Divine Saviour Himself has laid the foundation of the religious state, and established it in His Church by His teaching and His example. We need only open the Gospels to be convinced of this. The counsel of perfect obedience was given when our Divine Master said to His disciples, " If thou wilt be perfect . . . follow me : " but " if any man will come after me, let him deny himself."† The counsel of perfect chastity was given when our Lord praised those who voluntarily deprive themselves of all the pleasures of sense " for the king-

* 1 Pet. ii. 9. † Matt. xix. 21 ; xvi. 24.

dom of heaven's sake."* The counsel of perfect
poverty was given by our Saviour when He said,
" If thou wilt·be perfect, go sell what thou hast, and
give to the poor . . . and come, follow me."†
Although our Divine Master Jesus Christ addresses
these counsels to all the faithful, still He does not
oblige all to follow them, and even teaches us that
His Heavenly Father does not give to all the grace
to understand them. These counsels, therefore,
apply particularly to chosen souls whom our
Heavenly Father calls to a higher perfection.

I have said that our Lord has taught the evangelical counsels, not only by His discourses, but
also by His example. And, indeed, we see that He
practised in all circumstances a perfect obedience
both towards His Father in heaven and his parents
on earth. Holy Writ gives us warrant for saying
so. St. Luke remarks that in His childhood He was
submissive to Mary and to Joseph: "And He was
subject to them."‡ When His parents were astonished to find Him in the temple, He alleged as a
motive His obedience to God: "Did you not know,"
He said to them, "that I must be about my
Father's business?"§ In the Garden of Olives,
when broken with woe at the sight of His cruel
Passion, He cried out, "Father, . . . not my will,
but Thine be done." ‖ The Apostle assures us that
He was obedient unto death, and that for His obedience "God hath given Him a name which is above

* Matt. xix. 12.   † Ib. xix. 21.   ‡ Luke ii. 51.
        § Ib. ii. 49.   ‖ Ib. xxii. 42.

all names."* Again, our Divine Master has given an
example of perfect chastity by living in perpetual
virginity.   His purity was so dazzling that His
disciples were astonished even when He talked with
the Samaritan woman whom He wished to convert.† God permitted not His bitterest enemies to
calumniate His chastity, even though He allowed
them to calumniate His sobriety and His zeal.
Lastly, the perfect poverty which He professed
stands out in all the important circumstances of
His life.   Although a descendant of David, He was
born in Bethlehem, in a stable, poor and abandoned: as a child He lived in the workshop of a
poor artisan.   When the income-tax was demanded
from Him, He was obliged to work a miracle to
procure the means of paying it.   He declared that
He had not even a stone to lay His head on.   He
died stripped of all things.

Here then are the three evangelical counsels proclaimed, recommended and practised by our Saviour.
These counsels have been understood and followed
from their first origin: almost all our Saviour's disciples practised them in the earliest times and have
had imitators ever since.

But what is the aim, and, if I may so speak, the
economy of these counsels?   How do they lead us
to perfection?   How does their observance constitute a stage of perfect life?

To understand their aim and spirit we must
recall the fall of our nature and the weakness which

* Philipp. ii. 9.   † John iv. 27.

has been its consequence. The Apostle St. John reduces these weaknesses, when we are unable to get the better of them, to three vices or perverse inclinations: "For all that is in the world is the concupiscence of the flesh, and the concupiscence of the eyes, and the pride of life."* That is to say, all is either pride, or disorderly love of self; or else concupiscence of the flesh, or disorderly love of pleasures; or else concupiscence of the eyes, or disorderly love of honours, or of the perishable goods of this world. To these three fundamental vices of our nature our Lord opposes the three evangelical counsels, as infallible remedies, capable of removing these great obstacles to our salvation, and of replacing them by the practice of virtues which lead us without difficulty to our salvation. Let us now explain this truth.

Ever since the prevarication of Adam, who fell by pride and disobedience, all men bear in the depths of their souls a disorderly love of self, which of itself is enough to lead them into misfortune. By pride man disobeyed God and sinned, by pride he refuses obedience to his temporal or spiritual superiors, by pride he becomes unbearable to his brethren, by pride he oftentimes makes himself unbearable to himself. From this poisonous root of pride a hundred divers vices spring: it produces wrath, vengefulness, envy, jealousy, egotism; and, I may say, a man who is the slave of pride is capable of all excesses and of all crimes. Even for those

* 1 John ii. 16.

who do not give themselves up to the violent
inspirations of pride, this vice is still a dangerous enemy and a serious embarrassment. The
pleasure of doing one's own will blinds many of
the faithful, and blinds them concerning the rule
of their duties. This vice is so subtile that it glides
into the most pious souls and those most devoted
to God. It finds sustenance even in virtue and in
the most praiseworthy works; it infects and spoils
them in God's eyes by vain complaisance and contemplation of self, which Christian humility condemns and can never allow. The virtue of humility
is recommended to us as a remedy for this great
evil; and certainly it is sufficient to cure it, when
well practised: but how can this practice be easy
when we find around us and in us a thousand foods
for pride, a thousand provocatives to self-love?

Without doubt the most efficacious and easiest
means is to pluck up the evil by its root, to take
away from pride all its nourishment, to tie down
this imperious will under the yoke of evangelical
obedience, to make the vow of perfect and perpetual
obedience. This voluntary, deliberate and constant
submission cuts off at a blow from our natural pride,
not only every subject, but even every opportunity
of showing itself. It subordinates the will immediately to God and to the superiors who represent
Him, so that the religious who has set out on this
road can direct himself with the greatest security
in all his actions, just as if his spiritual advance-
ment were in the hands of our Lord Jesus Christ
Himself, or in those of his superiors. It is no longer

himself, in a manner, but those whom he obeys that
are responsible for his soul ; as for himself, he stops
at the simple obedience and goes no further.   Hence
a very lively sentiment of confidence, security and
peace, which the movements of pride cannot disturb,
and which leaves the soul in possession of all its
energies to raise itself towards God, and to cleave to
Him by rapid progress in the practice of virtue.
Such is the way in which perfect obedience delivers
us from the tyranny of pride.

Another obstacle to salvation and Christian perfection is to be found in the disorderly love of
sensible pleasures, in that fatal sensuality which
daily makes so many victims in the world and hurls
into hell so many unhappy ones.   Of this vice .the
Apostle speaks when he says that " the sensual man
perceiveth not these things that are of the Spirit of
God."*   He is the slave of his passions, he flatters
his senses, he dreams only of pleasure, and, if he
gives himself up to it, he degrades and ruins his
body and perverts his faculties, and in the end falls
into complete brutalization, unable to quench his
cruel and insatiable cravings.   Faithful souls,
quickened by the fear of God, feel horror, no doubt,
at this degradation ; but, despite their goodwill,
how many snares does not their virtue come across
in this world !   How many temptations, sieges,
perils !   What difficulty oftentimes in distinguish-
ing what is allowed and what is not !   What disquietude and remorse !   Satan's angel is there, and

* 1 Cor. ii. 14.

we don't always think of calling upon the angel of light, or else we lack strength and courage to follow his advice. The inward war which the corrupt senses wage against the will is a difficulty, an obstacle, an embarrassment in the path of salvation. The counsel of perfect chastity brings a remedy for this evil in a manner truly triumphant. At one blow it deprives the sensual appetites of their ordinary nourishment, it removes occasions, puts aside dangers, makes us shut our eyes to the figure of this fleeting world and fix them on the Spotless Lamb, our model : and thus inspires the love of perfect purity and holiness. By observing this counsel we consecrate our body to God, and offer it to Him as a living holocaust; we impose the strictest reserve upon our senses, make a covenant with our eyes, shun the approach of vice, and, with God's grace, lead the life of angels upon earth.

The third obstacle to salvation—disorderly love of riches and of the goods of this world—is no less to be feared by timorous souls than disorderly love of pleasure and of self. The disorders, crimes, pertur- bations of soul that the thirst for gold entails is something inexpressible. " For they that will become rich," says the Apostle, " fall into tempta- tion, and into the snare of the devil, and into many unprofitable and hurtful desires, which drown men into destruction and perdition."* " No covetous person," he says again, "hath inheritance in the

---

* 1 Tim. vi. 9.   † Eph. v. 5 ; cf. 1. Cor. vi. 10.
‡ 1 Cor. vi. 9.

kingdom of Christ and of God."† Elsewhere he
condemns the unjust.‡ Our Saviour ranks among
the condemned those who refused a share of their
goods to the poor. He shows the fate reserved for
the slaves of earthly goods in the history of the
wicked rich man for whom Lazarus, after his death,
could not even procure a drop of water. They who
are prodigal of their goods and ruin their family are
no less guilty than those who amass goods beyond
all moderation and by all means possible. Thus sin
may be committed both in striving to gain them, in
possessing them, in hoarding them, and in squan-
dering them. If a thing is not used according to
God's will, or if the heart is attached to it, everything is a danger and an occasion of fall. As to
the faithful who keep themselves free from sordid
avarice, from spendthrift folly, and from the excesses
which love of earthly goods so often entails, even
they find in the possession of these goods at least a
source of disquietude which turns away their
thoughts from their eternal interests, and afterwards
hopes and anxieties which retard their advance in
the path of virtue : a real embarrassment, indeed, in
the practice of piety. Now the evangelical counsel
of perfect poverty removes at once all these difficulties and snares. It gives back to the will its balance
and its dominion by disentangling it for ever from
the goods of earth, and leaving it only its desire for
the goods of heaven. It cuts off for good and all
the use of things superfluous, and regulates the use
of necessary ones, not leaving us a free disposal of
them ; and so forestalls all desires and disquietude.

The fear of losing and the hope of gaining have no more entrance into the heart, because it is quite detached from the goods of earth, and only aspires to those of heaven.

Thus our Saviour has opposed to the three most fruitful sources of our sins and' vices three sources of good thoughts, good sentiments and good deeds. To native and hereditary pride He opposes perfect obedience; to sensuality and concupiscence He opposes perfect chastity; and to avarice and ambition He opposes perfect poverty. Now we shall understand how the observance of the three evangelical counsels frees the souls who vow themselves thereto from that slavery of vice in which the worldling groans, and procures for them the true liberty of the children of God. Disburdened by the operation of these Divine virtues from the weight of corrupt nature, which weighs down all mortal men, and placed under the influence of grace, a soul lifts herself towards God without effort and, as it were, of herself. As the vessel, whose cargo is light and whose sails are wide, rapidly cleaves the waves and soon makes the harbour, the soul of him who has embraced the evangelical counsels advances with rapid steps in the path of Christian perfection, and easily makes her way to God. For, on the one hand, nothing keeps back, slackens, or hinders her advance; and, on the other, grace no longer finds in her any obstacle or resistance; and so everything works together for her perfection, to which she thus arrives without violence or struggle.

The observance of these counsels, if only for a while, could not produce all these advantages; it is only fruitful in case it be perpetual, or at least constant. They who embrace these counsels by choice, in obedience to the voice of their conscience and the voice of God, generally oblige themselves thereto by a solemn promise which binds them for ever. The *vows*—for thus this promise is called— are sacred fetters which the will puts upon itself in order to forearm itself against the effects of natural inconstancy; by pronouncing them the soul binds herself in a secret and holy slavery which increases the merit of the good she does. In fact, the will is stronger when it is bound, and its sacrifice is more perfect, because more secure. It is thus more pleasing to God. A simple comparison will be sufficient to prove this: is it not true that, by taking upon oneself the livery of a prince, and by obliging oneself to serve him all one's life, a stricter attachment is thereby formed with him, we become dearer to him, and have more right to his munifi- cence, than those who serve him rarely and without any such strict obligation?

It is by pronouncing the vows that the observ- ance of the evangelical counsels acquires a perfect steadfastness and becomes a state of life properly so called, viz., the *religious state.*

It is not without reason that the manner of life of those faithful who have embraced the con- stant practice of the evangelical counsels is called the " religious state," or " the state of perfection." All Christians, without doubt, are obliged, by virtue of their Baptism, to live religiously, that is, to observe God's law, and to pay Him the worship which is due to His Divine Majesty ; but they do not live exclusively for God and for religion. Their business, their duties as fathers of families, as members of civil society, absorb a great part of their thoughts and demand a large share of their time. On the contrary, those who vow themselves to the practice of the evangelical counsels reserve nothing either of themselves or of their time. God possesses them without reserve and disposes of them, in all respects, according to His good pleasure. They are therefore *religious* by excellence, in the full meaning of the word. They are religious by their state, by profession. They practise the virtue of religion in its highest perfection ; they bind themselves to God by the strongest, holiest, most lasting ties ; they offer themselves up to God as victims of sweet savour, and in all things seek but the worship and glory of God.

This state is also called the *state of perfection*, and not without a motive is it thus qualified. It is true that all the faithful are called to a certain perfection by the observance of the precepts or commands of God. "The precepts," says St. Thomas,* "have for their chief object the love of God and of our neighbour ; a love in which is found the very essence of Christian perfection. This love, according to St. Paul,† is 'the bond of perfection,' that is to say, the principle by which all other virtues

* Opuscul. xvii. 6.   † Col. iii. 14.

are brought into relation with God, and combine to attach the soul to God. It is, therefore, certain that the precepts lead to perfection. But the counsels lead thitherward after another manner. The precepts, in the sense that if we do not observe them we shall not attain our end; the counsels, in the sense that by their aid we attain this end more easily and more surely." The state of perfection, therefore, does not bear this name in the sense that all who enter it must be perfect, or that all who embrace it are so in reality; but it is thus called because it removes, more efficaciously than all other states of life, the obstacles to perfection, and furnishes the most numerous and efficacious means to attain to perfection speedily. Not only does the religious state contain many means of perfection peculiar to itself—such as the rule, the habit, the example of brethren, the counsels and directions of superiors— but we may also say that the greater part of the ordinary means of perfection employed in the world are found in their full perfection in this holy state. So, for instance, prayer, fasting, almsdeeds, which the ordinary faithful practise in obedience to God's commandments and the precept of the Gospel, acquire in the religious life a degree of perfection which they have not in the practice of common life. The simple faithful every day say some short prayers; the religious pray a great part of the night and day. Prayer bends the soul to God; the perfect obedience which the religious adds to it submits the entire man to God. Fasting mortifies the body. In the world people fast during Lent, at the Embertimes, on vigils. In the cloister they fast during Advent also, during the Monastic Lent, on other days besides; and to the fast add perfect chastity, which subjugates all the senses in order to submit them to God. In the world people give alms, they grant the poor a small share of their goods, and this share is given successively and in small instalments. In the cloister all goods are given up at once, in order to embrace perfect poverty. It is the same with the practice of the virtues, which, in the cloister, is easier, more steadfast, and leads more surely to perfection. Lastly, let us add, that if a man is not perfect when he embraces this state, he must, nevertheless, nourish in his heart an ardent desire to arrive speedily at perfection.

He who enters the religious state, hath heard and understood the counsel of our Heavenly Father, who was inviting him to holy solitude to the perfect life. He hath obeyed that invitation of our Saviour: "Come ye after me."* He walks in the footsteps of his Divine Master, and if he be faithful to his vocation he is certain to arrive at happiness.

From what we have said, every one may see how holy and valuable a thing is vocation to the religious state.

* Matt. iv. 19.

CHAPTER XII.

*Of the Different Religious Orders to which one may
be called.*

THE religious life founded in the Church by our
Lord Jesus Christ has been the same in all ages as
regards its substance ; but in its outward form and
practice it has varied, in order to answer better the
ends of Divine Providence and the needs of souls.
We will in this chapter attempt a brief sketch of it.

The evangelical counsels were practised in the
beginning by isolated members of the faithful, who
stopped at home, under their father's roof, and in
the bosom of their family.   Later on, and especially
in the times of the persecutions, many Christians
fled into solitary spots or into deserts, in order to
lead therein a more perfect life, far away from the
din and bustle of the world.   When their numbers
became pretty considerable they were called *monks*
or *solitaries*, because they lived isolated, alone, in a
hut, or in the cleft of a rock.   On account of their
retiring from the cities they were also called *anchorites*, which signifies men *retired* from inhabited
places.

When they began to gather together into monasteries, in order to lead a life in common, they were
styled *cenobites*, that is, people living in common ;
whilst those who dwelt in the desert received the
name of *hermits*, from the place of their dwelling.

Persons of the female sex who embraced the

monastic life were known under the name of *virgins*,
widows, or *deaconesses*. From the earliest times
they received the veil, as a sign of the consecration
they made of themselves to God; they could not
quit this holy state, after having once embraced it,
without being considered sacrilegious.

In the earliest ages the religious had no other
occupation than prayer and manual labour. They
were admitted very soon to the priesthood, but they
hardly busied themselves in anything but works of
charity, except under extraordinary circumstances,
such as public calamities or the ravages of heresy.
Then they quitted their deserts, and came into the
cities to tend and console the sick, or else to refute
heresies and strengthen the faithful in the faith.

The religious life, which was very widespread in
the East, even at the time of the persecutions,
extended greatly in the West, after the circulation of the beautiful life of St. Antony, written
by St. Athanasius, Patriarch of Alexandria, for the
edification of the faithful. Egypt, the Thebaiid,
the deserts of Nitriæ, became famous throughout the world, and Christians of all countries
were to be seen coming into the midst of these
nations of saints, in order to form themselves more
easily in the practice of the religious life. *The
Lives of the Fathers of the Desert*, still read in
Christian families, are well calculated to develope a
taste for the perfect life, and to bring to blossom
vocations to the religious state.

In the East it was St. Basil who stamped the
monastic institutions with their definite form. In

the West St. Benedict became the patriarch of the religious life, to which he gave a new lustre. His rule has always been considered as the basis of the new constitutions which the needs of the times have given rise to since. His disciples have been for centuries the most perfect models of the perfect life. Ever since their foundation they have united to the exercises of their rule and the austerity of their virtues the study of sacred literature, the education of youth, and preaching. For nearly a thousand years they were the glory and the joy of the Church. Nowadays, as they are rising again from their ashes, they are the object of the most consoling hopes.

At the beginning of the thirteenth century St. Francis of Assisi founded the order of Friars Minors, who have professed from the beginning to practise evangelical poverty in its highest perfection. At the same time St. Dominic founded the order of Friars Preachers, to combat heresy and to defend the faith in the countries where it was attacked. These two Orders made rapid increase, and caused the religious life to flourish with a success hitherto almost unknown.

In the sixteenth and seventeenth centuries religious orders multiplied afresh, in order to repair the ruins that had been piled up by the pretended " Reformation." Some chose as the object of their labours the apostolic life and the preaching of the faith ; others the Christian education of youth ; others, again, works of charity, the consolation of the sick, of lunatics, of orphans, and of the unfortunates of all descriptions.

Among these religious orders the most celebrated
of all is the Company of Jesus, founded by St.
Ignatius of Loyola. This institution may be compared to those rivers which are able to carry vessels
even at their very source. The first companions
of the holy founder worked wonders in the Church.
St. Francis Xavier, the Apostle of the Indies and
the *Thaumaturgus* of his age, was himself enough
to make illustrious for ever the Order which produced him. Other sons of St. Ignatius proclaimed
the faith in all the countries of the world, and
received in great numbers the palm of martyrdom.
Those, too, who have devoted themselves to the
education of youth, or have defended the Church
by their pen, are to be reckoned by thousands.
This Order has, moreover, the distinguished honour
to have merited at all times the hatred and persecution of the enemies of truth and virtue.

In these latter times St. Alphonsus de' Liguori,
Bishop of Sant' Agata, has founded an apostolic
order under the patronage of our Blessed Redeemer
(Redemptorists). At first the religious of this
Order devoted themselves to preaching in the
country, as formerly did the sons of St. Norbert;
now they give themselves to the apostleship under
all forms. God has made them in our days powerful
instruments of His mercy.

The Orders of women have constantly followed
the progress and development of the religious
orders of men. This is not, however, the place to
speak of them.

This short review of the monastic orders founded

in the Church proves that the religious state, always the same in its essence, has put on different forms at different epochs, and has always adapted itself to the wants of the Church and the necessities of the time.

In order to accommodate themselves thus to the exigencies of the moment, the religious orders have adapted particular rules and practices suited to the object of their institution. Each of these families has become a distinct *Order*, and has worked good in a particular sphere. Love of God and of their neighbour have been the soul of them all ; but Divine charity has been exercised in their hearts by means of different works. All the Orders have been ornaments, helps, means of edification to the Church ; their very existence attests the presence of the Holy Spirit, who alone can develope vocations to the perfect state and the empire of grace which sways the heart : all have contributed in their own way to the triumph of faith and of Christian virtues.

It does not belong to our plan to recount the immense benefits received from them by Christian peoples, for such details would lead us too far. It suffices to remark here that all religious orders may be divided into two classes, viz., those Orders which have for their end the *contemplative* life, and those which have for their end the *active* life. The Orders which seem to belong at one and the same time to both classes will form, if you like, a third class, which adopts the mixed life, or may be ranged in one of the two preceding classes, according to the spirit and the exercises predominant in them.

It is very certain that God calls many young people to one of these lives, to the exclusion of the other. Let us explain in a few words their nature and properties.

Those are called *contemplative* orders which impose complete solitude and enclosure, which subject the body more perfectly to God by great austerities, and which, by the exercise of prayer and meditation, lead the mind and the heart directly to a more intimate union with God. Contemplation is but a fervent and sublime prayer which raises the soul to God with a single impulse; it is an intellectual and effective consideration of the greatness, goodness, beauty, justice, mercy, and other attributes of the Creator and Redeemer of men; it is a profound and steadfast meditation upon the works of God which invites and aids all the powers of the soul to adore, admire and praise God; it is a prelude on earth to the adoration and praises to be one day offered to God, in company with the blessed, in heaven.

The contemplative life is also ancient in the Church: the holy Fathers have spoken of it at all times. In our age of coldness and indifference many souls touched by grace feel so lively, so violent an attraction for this holy and beautiful state, that they think themselves the unhappiest of creatures when they cannot enter it. What we read in the lives of several saints, that God seemed to pursue them and to draw them to Himself by an irresistible force, frequently happens even in our days. If any one doubt it, let him visit one of our monasteries

wherein this holy life is practised. He will see with
his own eyes that there is not on earth a state
sweeter or happier than that in which souls apply
themselves to mortify the senses, to deny themselves perfectly, to practise Divine charity, and to
enjoy the advantages and delights of holy contemplation.   People in the world can't understand
at all this all-heavenly manner of living : they hardly
suspect its existence, and certainly do not understand its value.   Libertines and unbelievers blame
and attack it as a foolery ; but souls which have
tasted it would not exchange it for all the treasures
of the world.   But wherefore make its panegyric
here ?   The carnal man will not understand our
reasonings better than he understands the things of
God, and the spiritual man will believe without
difficulty his own eyes and our experience.

The contemplative life peopled Egypt with saints
and heaven with the elect.   Happy the souls whom
God calls thereunto by His grace, and whom He
causes to persevere to the end !   These souls are for
the rest of the faithful a moving subject of edification, and themselves enjoy by anticipation the
bliss of heaven.

The religious orders, which have for their end the
works of the active life, are also very great in the
eyes of faith.   They are organized in such a manner
that the exercises of piety practised therein prepare
their subjects for the extensive works which the
Order is especially called to accomplish.   We have
already indicated these works and marked out their
aim.   The propagation of the faith among infidel

nations, preaching amid Christian peoples, the instruction and education of youth, the care of the
sick, the infirm, orphans, abandoned children—in
fact, all the works inspired to generous hearts by
the twofold love of God and of our neighbour, are
so many holy undertakings which active religious
orders set before themselves, and generally lead to a
successful issue.

The usefulness of these Orders in the Church is
manifest. God accomplishes by their ministry a
host of works that would never have been done had
these Orders not existed. Their mission is a noble
and a great one, worthy of the ambition of a
Christian heart. God calls many young men and
women to this active religious life also, and grants
them the grace of sanctifying themselves therein,
whilst at the same time working wonders that the
world is astonished at, and which heresy envies us.
Happy those chosen souls, too, whom God destines
to the fulfilling of these works, and to whom He has
specially promised a crown of glory and happiness
without end!

We shall, perhaps, be asked which of these two
lives—the contemplative or the active—appears preferable. In theory this question is almost idle; in
practice, God ordinarily decides specially for each
subject. Still, we may say that if the contemplative life appears sublimer in itself, because it
tends more directly to God and knits the contemplative soul more closely to God; still the active
life appears more useful to the Church on account
of the noble and great works it accomplishes. Thus

a balance is preserved between them. At the same time it must be acknowledged that on the one hand the contemplative life is sovereignly useful to the Church, both by the benefits it procures for the faithful who embrace it, and by the edification it causes to those of the faithful who do not devote themselves to it, as well as by the prayers it incessantly offers to God for the spiritual and temporal welfare of His people ; as, on the other hand, the active life is sublime, both because of the sentiment of charity that quickens it, and by reason of the great deeds it works.

These two kinds of life are, therefore, holy and sublime ; and whatever be the choice at which you arrive, after having well examined the case in God's presence, you may be sure to have chosen in the spiritual inheritance the better part, like Mary.

CHAPTER XIII.

Of Vocation to the Religious State.

To the general idea of Divine vocation which we have given in the earlier chapters, it is fitting to add in this place some special remarks on the peculiar character of vocation to the religious state, and on the signs that indicate it.

If we take literally the words of the Gospel, in which our Saviour invites us to embrace the perfect life, it would appear that all men without exception are invited to this state. Our Divine Saviour says.

to us: " If thou wilt be perfect, go sell what thou hast and give to the poor, . . . and come, follow me."* He says, "If thou would'st be perfect," speaking to everybody: nobody is excluded, every one may embrace this state, if he wish; hence this career is open to all the world. And indeed how could it be closed? Ought not the state of perfection to be, if not the share, at least the desire of every one? Wherefore should God have forbidden to anybody that state in which are to be met fewer obstacles to salvation and more means to arrive thereat? The general invitation that our Saviour addresses to all the faithful, and the idea which He gives us of the religious state, might lead us to think that there is on God's part a universal vocation to the religious state, a vocation which obliges all Christians, in a indeterminate and conditional manner, without there being for anybody a special vocation that obliges strictly. And yet this is not the case.

The invitation which our Divine Master addresses to all does not exclude the formal order that He gives to many. We hold it for certain that we must here distinguish three dispositions of Divine Providence. To a small number of the faithful He forbids entrance into the religious state; on a certain number of others He imposes it; whilst to the greatest number He offers it, but leaving them a perfect liberty to embrace it as soon as ever they feel any attraction for it. Let us explain these three cases.

To begin with, it is evident that Providence

* Matt. xix. 21.

excludes, for the time being, from the religious state, all the faithful who have taken to another state, whose duties are incompatible with the exercises of the religious life. Thus married people, or those who are obliged to stay in the world to care for the support of their parents or children, or those who live under the authority of another and have not free disposal of their own will, such as were slaves in former times, and nowadays still are minors, cannot enter the religious state, as long as they are kept in the world by impediments of this kind.

God also excludes from the religious life such Christians as are not disposed to submit to the exercises of this state, whether through defect of a good will, or on account of the tyranny of their passions or evil habits, which make them incapable of bending to the yoke of monastic rule and obedience. A heart that is strayed or hardened cannot love solitude and penance. To engage in this state without being prepared for it, and without being able to profit by the advantages it presents and the consolations it promises, is to hurl oneself into an abyss, to doom oneself to perdition. However perfect it be, this state can never become useful and advantageous to those who do not understand and are not prepared for it. A sick person cannot bear the food given him, however substantial it may be : energetic remedies kill those patients who have not strength to digest them.

There are also certain persons, ecclesiastics for instance, who feel themselves inwardly called to the religious state, and who yet cannot follow this inward vocation immediately, because if they were to do so they would cause considerable loss to the Church, or would gravely offend their superiors. Canon Law has provided for cases in which an ecclesiastic is permitted to quit the world precipitately in order to enter the religious state, whatsover be the dignities and functions with which he is invested, and even in spite of the refusal of his superiors; but such cases are rare and require to be very well established before they can be admitted. Common prudence points out another way. When a man hears in his inmost heart a Divine voice calling him to the perfect life, whilst outward ties, which he cannot break without preventing a great good or causing a certain evil, hold him back in the world, let him address himself with confidence and simplicity to his superiors, whose lights are well known, and whose consciences are involved in the case, in order to obtain direction and advice. If they allow him to follow immediately the inclination of his heart, well and good. For the rest, he must not disquiet himself any more: if they think, before God, that he ought to wait, let him have a little patience and resignation, remembering that he obeys God by obeying those who hold His place here below. God has two manners of manifesting His holy will: one in the soul, by His grace; the other in the ear, by the voice of superiors. When there is any doubt or appearance of conflict between these two manifestations of God's will, the second is always the surest.

Let us now pass on to the second case, in which
a Christian is rigorously bound to enter the religious
state. This case is more frequent and more practical than people think.

To begin with, there are certain friends of God,
whom He inspires with so lively a desire of consecrating themselves to Him and so violent an attraction to embrace the perfect life, that they cannot
resist it without offending His goodness and His
love. The pressing invitation that they feel incessantly echoing in the depths of their soul, imposes upon them a sort of necessity of obeying. It
is equivalent to an order, or a precept. To stifle
or despise this manifestation of God's will, is evidently to expose oneself to the danger of displeasing
God, and of breaking the chain of grace, by which
He draws this soul to Himself, and of losing for
life those powerful and conquering graces which
lead securely to salvation.

There are others of the faithful who, endowed
with a feeble and flitting will, are overruled by
strong and tyrannizing passions, so long as they
are without the support and counsel of a devoted
guide. The consciousness of their weakness dis-
quiets them. The desire of working out their
salvation with confidence preoccupies them. The
religious state alone offers them, in the practice of
mortification and penance, a remedy for their
passions, and in the practice of obedience a solid
support for their will. Let these ardent and yet
feeble characters venture in the midst of the dangers
of the world, they will rush into excesses and cause

their own misfortune. Let them submit themselves to the yoke of the perfect life, and they will work wonders, whilst at the same time they will preserve the peace and calm which is to cause their happiness.

If a Christian constantly meet in the world a proximate occasion of offending God, an occasion which he can only put aside by consecrating himself to the religious life, he also will evidently be obliged to embrace this life.

Hence it is certain that many of the faithful who would lose themselves in the world are saved in the cloister. This is the doctrine of St. Gregory the Great. This illustrious Pope begged of Maurice, the Emperor of Constantinople, to revoke the law by which he forbade the monasteries ever to receive state officers who had exercised civil functions, or had been attached to the army. He implored the emperor to revoke this law, for fear it should become a cause of eternal loss to Christians who could only save themselves by embracing the monastic life.* His conviction on this point was profound, for he again expresses it in his homilies on the Holy Gospels, wherein he says: "Many there are who, unless they abandon all things, can by no means be saved before God."†

Beyond these two classes of the faithful, some of whom may not embrace the religious life, whilst the others are obliged to enter it, there is a great multitude in the Church to whom our Saviour

---

* Epistles, bk. iii., ep. 65, vol. ii., col. 676.   † Hom. 37.

addresses a general invitation and leaves a free
choice. It is to them properly that He says : " If
thou wilt, come after me!" You may save yourselves in the world, but you will save yourselves
more surely and more easily in the cloister. I do
not impose any precept upon you : only I give you
a counsel.

If we are asked why our Divine Master has pronounced this general invitation, why He has said :
"If thou wilt, follow me!" we shall not hesitate to
answer that He has wished to give us to understand, first, that He Himself opposes no obstacle to
this manner of life, that He throws open, as far as
depends on Him, this easy way to salvation to all
the faithful, although several, either by their own
fault or by force of circumstances, are either incapable or unworthy of embracing it. He also wished
to teach us that the choice of this state of life does
not ordinarily require a long deliberation, so favourable is it to the sanctification of souls and the con-
quest of the kingdom of God. Lastly, He teaches
us by this general invitation that the religious state
is suited to a great number of the faithful, and that
persons of all ages, all ranks, and every kind of
merit, may enter therein in order to better achieve
their salvation. This latter fact is so noteworthy as
to deserve special notice in this place.

We see in the history of the Church that there is
no class of the faithful which has not embraced and
practised the religious life. Not only young men
and women who have arrived at the age for chosing
a state of life, but children of a tender age, old

people, widowers and widows, married people,
either together or separately, have been received
into monasteries, and led therein a perfect life.
Noble and rich, poor men and slaves, great and
little, priests and layfolk, magistrates and artisans,
princes, soldiers and their servants, great sinners
and innocent souls have successively sought shelter
and found refuge therein. There is no state or
condition which has not sent some of its members
to the religious life.

Entering into details, I notice, to begin with,
that in the monasteries of both East and West
those sweet and benevolent words of our Saviour
have been taken literally :—" Suffer the little
children to come unto me, and forbid them
not."* Hence young children have been received,
when presented by their parents or by themselves.
They have been taught sacred letters from the
tenderest age, in order that they might be like
Timothy, whom St. Paul congratulates on having
learnt them in his infancy.† St. Basil, the
patriarch of the monks of the East, in his monastic
constitutions, orders children to be received from
the tenderest age; and that, when they arrive at
the age of reason, they be admitted to the voluntary
profession, or else sent away, in the presence of
witnesses. "At the time of making their profession," says he, "let them make for some days the
spiritual exercises in a separate cell, in order to deliberate on their future state of life."‡ St. Benedict,

* Mark x. 14.　　† 2 Tim, iii. 15.
‡ Regula fusius disputata, xv.

the patriarch of the monks of the West, also orders
in his rule (chap. lix. and lxx.) that children be
received into the monasteries and enrolled in the
sacred ranks. The Church fixed the age at which
these children could be admitted to voluntary profession, first at ten years, afterwards at fourteen, and
lastly, in the Council of Trent, at sixteen years. St.
John Chrysostom extols this custom very much, because, he says, children are more docile, and let themselves be trained easily to the monastic life, in which
they are afterwards happy for the rest of their days.
It is not without reason that to this practice of receiving children in monasteries are attributed the great
works which religious orders performed in the
Middle Ages for the welfare of nations and the glory
of the Church. The bulk of the great statesmen,
great saints, and great writers which the order of
St. Benedict produced in its most flourishing epoch,
had been admitted from their tenderest years into
the cloister, where they had grown up under the
shadow of the altar.

Monastic life also admits the aged. After long
years passed in the world amid the whirl of business
and the dreams of ambition, souls touched by grace
seek at the close of their life the repose of solitude
and the quietness of the cloister, in order to prepare
better for death. St. Ephrem frequently insists on
the obligation of monasteries to receive aged persons
who present themselves.*   Palladius, in the *Lives
of the Fathers of the Desert*, narrates that St.

* St. Ephrem: *Works*, p. 288, 516, 770, ed. Colon.

Antony received among his disciples an old man of
sixty years called Paul.* St. Gregory of Nazianzus
declares that a certain Eudoxius is all the more fit
to embrace the religious life, inasmuch as the frosts
of old age have more perfectly extinguished in him
the fire of the passions.† Pelagius tells the history
of two old men who entered a monastery together
with their young children, in order to serve God for
the rest of their days.‡ These examples are not
rare in the annals of early times, nor are they rare
even in our times. Further on we will cite several
facts of this kind.

The faithful who are engaged in marriage may
disengage themselves, in order to embrace the perfect life. It has always been held in the Church that
married persons who have no duties to perform
towards their family, or who have provided sufficiently for them, may retire, with common consent,
from the trammels of secular life—the husband into
a monastery of men, and the wife into a convent of
women, in order to live therein the perfect life.
This law is so general, it has been so often applied,
that the Church has inserted it in her code of Canon
Law.|| Let it be well remarked that it is not
permitted for one of the parties to retire without
the consent of the other; but as soon as the two

* Palladius : *Hist. Lausiac.*
† St. Gregory Naz. *Ep.* 178, vol. ii., p. 146, ed. Bened.
‡ Pelagius : lib. v., no. 21—22.
|| Alexander III., c. *Cum Sis*, De Conversat. Coniug. and
c. *Prœterea*, ib. The Canonists in chap. *Quidam* and c.
Verum, ib. See also St. Gregory the Great : *Epistles*, bk.
vi., ep. 48, vol. ii., col. 827.

M

parties are agreed, and the other conditions fulfilled, the Church no longer puts any obstacle to their entering religion.

How many illustrious widows have waited only for the death of their husbands, in order to consecrate themselves entirely to God! St. Jerome narrates with admiration the self-denial of a great number of Roman ladies, amongst whom are distinguished St. Paula and St. Melania.* The annals of the Middle Ages and those of these latter days mark out for our especial veneration St. Elizabeth of Hungary, St. Frances of Rome, and St. Jane Frances Chantal.

How many nobles, rich men, politicians, and great warriors have exchanged their treasures for monastic poverty, their dignities for the humility of the cloister, their authority and their office for evangelical obedience! St. Arsenius, before flying into holy solitude, had ruled the Empire of the East. Cassiodorus had been a senator and prefect or governor of a province when he put on the religious habit. Charles V., the most powerful monarch of his time, wished to die in the serge habit, and passed his last years in the exercise of religious virtues. St. Francis Borgia, whose example he loved to quote, had preceded him in this path of humility and self-denial. At the beginning of this century Charles Emmanuel, King

---

* St. Jerome: ep. 39 *(on the Death of Blesilla)* ; ep. 66 *(Panegyric of Paulina)* ; ep. 108 *(Epitaph of Paula)* ; ep. 127 *(Epit. of the Widow Marcella to the Virgin Principia).*

of Sardinia, laid aside his royal purple, and died a simple Jesuit lay-brother in the professed house in Rome.

Side by side with kings are ranged in the cloister men of humble rank, the disinherited, and even slaves. The poor, artizans, soldiers, or workpeople, who feel themselves called by God to the perfect life, have never been repulsed from the monastery. It is only required that they be free and able to dispose of their persons. Thus slaves could not embrace the religious state without the consent of their masters. An ancient historian tells us that a slave who had become a religious in Egypt went up every year to Alexandria in order to thank his masters for having given him permission to embrace the religious life, and also to pay them a little recompense that he had promised them.* We read in the letters of St. Gregory the Great that the slaves of the Roman Church became free as soon as they wished to embrace the religious state.† "See you not," says St. Augustine, "of what a humble rank many persons are who come to monasteries, and who cannot be refused admittance without grave sin?"‡ When the Emperor Maurice, as we have already remarked, in order to prevent abuses, had forbidden soldiers, as well as civil officers who had not faithfully given in their accounts, to enter monasteries, St. Gregory begged

* Pelagius: bk. xv., no. 31.

† St. Gregory the Great: *Epistles*, bk. v., ep. 34, vol. ii., col. 761.

‡ St. Augustine: *Of the Work of Monks*, c. 22, vol vi., col. 492.

the Emperor either to soften the rigour of his law
or to abrogate it, and to allow the monasteries to
undertake the task of settling these affairs. In
support of his request, he says that these soldiers
and functionaries often arrive at a high degree of
perfection in the exercise of the religious life, and
that many of them who become saints therein would
be lost if they remained in the world.

Whatever the world think of it, it is certain that
the Church also receives great sinners into the
cloister, in order that they may do penance therein,
and make up for their crimes by the exercise of
heroic virtue. On this point there is a general law
of the Church, cited at the end of the Acts of the
Sixth Ecumenical Council, held in Constantinople
in 681, the terms of which I will quote: "It is
permitted to every Christian, of whatsoever crimes
he be known to be guilty, to embrace the religious
life, to fly the temptations of the world, to shut
himself up in a monastery, and to receive the
monastic tonsure. Our Saviour hath said that He
will reject no one who cometh to Him, and since
He hath described the life of penance under the
form of the monastic life, we felicitate those who
embrace it and never put any obstacle to the fulfilment of their desires."* This practice has been
constantly followed. St. Bernard attests it when
he says: " We receive *all* into monasteries, in the

---

* Harduin : *Acts of Councils*, t. iii., col. 1678, can. 43,
conc. in Trullo; ap. Nebrid. à Mundelheim, *Antiq. Mon.*,
p. 96.

hope of making them better."* And in our own
days we have seen great sinners retire, in an
admirable spirit of penance, into monasteries of the
Cistercian or Carthusian orders. The holy doctors
are agreed on this point that the religious state is
a state of penance, that it recalls the public penance
of the first ages of the Church, and that it is a
substitute for it for great sinners. St. Thomas
cites several decisions of the Sovereign Pontiffs,
who, having to judge concerning great sinners
guilty of public crimes, have given them the option
of embracing the monastic life, or of submitting to
a severe and long penance. In fact, the religious
life, especially in the austere orders, is a life of continual sacrifice and mortification, an uninterrupted
expiation of the sins of the past life. As several
religious orders nowadays give themselves up to
the apostleship and the sacred ministry, it is impossible for them to receive public sinners. But,
besides the active orders, all whose members must
enjoy a good reputation, there are also monasteries
into which great sinners may retire without incon-
venience, and enjoy in peace and silence all the
advantages of the religious life.

From the fact that sinners are received into
austere orders, it does not follow, as a false pre-
judice would make believe, that pure and innocent
souls must be excluded from them. The penitent
life befits the just as well as sinners, for penance is
just as efficacious in preventing sin as it is merit-

* St. Bernard: *De Consid.*, bk. iv., cap. iv., no. 11.

orious in expiating it. Besides, God calls young men
and women, who have been preserved in their first
innocence, to the practice of perfect virtue in the
most austere orders : and it is impossible to say for
what reason He should not call them.   Is not
penance a Christian virtue, common to all the
faithful, and the practice of which in all its degrees
is glorious and merit-worthy ?   Did not our Lord
Jesus Christ, although incapable of sin, do penance
for us ?   Wherefore after this may not innocent
souls offer themselves to God as holocausts or
expiating victims for the sins of their brethren,
and in order to increase their own holiness ?   Penance has the twofold virtue of satisfying for sins
committed and fortifying the soul against the
temptations of the devil, the world and the flesh.
The more the soul detaches herself from earth by
the renouncing of things earthly and the mortification of the senses, the more easily she raises herself
to God and the more closely she cleaves to Him.
Nothing, therefore, prevents young people of pure
and innocent life from being received into austere
orders.

It is also certain that there is no obstacle to
passing from the secular into the religious life.
The laws of the Church permit ecclesiastics, when
called of God to the perfect life, to quit their benefices and employments.   With due regard to
authority and the counsels of Christian prudence,
which we have already made mention of, ecclesiastics can, in certain cases, give up their functions,
notwithstanding their superiors, and engage them-

selves in the ways of the perfect life, breaking
through all ties which seem to chain them to the
world. Yet, in order to do this, we must be well
assured of the clear will of God, and that we are
quite safe from all illusion. In defence of this
principle several noteworthy instances may be
cited. St. Celestine V., who had been elevated
to the Sovereign Pontificate in difficult times,
abdicated the Apostolic See, laid aside the tiara,
and resumed, in the solitude of the cloister, the
exercises of the monastic life that he had quitted
with regret. In the reign of Benedict XIV. a
Vicar-General of the celebrated Cardinal Quirini,
Bishop of Brescia, although at the age of sixty,
entered the Society of Jesus against the Cardinal's wish. The latter believed himself unable
to do without his services in the administration
of his diocese; he wished, therefore, to compel
him to resume his functions. But Benedict XIV.,
being questioned upon the matter, after having
convinced himself that the vocation of this ecclesiastic was fully decided, pronounced in his favour,
and decided that the Cardinal must dispense with
a subject whom God so manifestly called to a more
perfect state.

Lastly, in our own days, Cardinal Odescalchi
voluntarily resigned the purple, renounced his
rich benefices, laid aside the exalted posts he
held in the administration of the Universal
Church, and took the humble habit of a novice
in the Society of Jesus. His sacrifice was not
of long duration. This pious cardinal, whom I

had the happiness to know, to love and to admire in Rome, and from whose hands I received my first orders, including the sub-deaconate, entered the noviciate on December 6th, 1838, and died in the odour of sanctity at Ferrara, of which city he had been archbishop, on the 17th of August, 1841.

The examples we have recalled prove, with evidence quite decisive, that the general invitation addressed by our Lord Jesus Christ to all His disciples has been understood and accepted by all classes of the faithful, under all conditions, and at all ages. At all times the effects of these Divine words, echoing constantly in the Church, have been visible:—"If thou wilt be perfect, go sell what thou hast, and give to the poor, and come, follow me." It is, therefore, certain that the invitation to the religious life is universal; that God makes it penetrate into souls, and renders it efficacious. It belongs, con-sequently, to the Providential government of the Church and the great work of the sanctification of men.

Happy the faithful to whom God grants this part of His inheritance; for, if they answer His advances, they begin to lead, even in this world, the life of the angels and the saints, and thus receive on earth a special warrant of their future happiness in heaven.

CHAPTER XIV.

Of the Principal Signs of Vocation to the Religious State.

A PIOUS author who published a few years ago a very useful book on the nature and duties of the monastic life, under the title of *Traite de l'Etat Religieux* ("Treatise on the Religious State"), reduces the signs of vocation to the religious life to two principal ones ; *fitness* and *attraction*.

Fitness consists in a disposition of body and soul proper for the exercise of the religious practices of the Order one desires to enter. It has, therefore, relation to the special duties which each rule imposes. " Whoever," says Father Gautrelet," desires to tend towards perfection, to subject himself to a rule, and to bind himself by vows with a view to this object ; whoever hopes to be able to practise the vows of poverty, chastity and obedience, and gives sufficient guarantees on this point ; provided there be nothing else in his physical or moral condition which really stands in the way of the fulfilment of his design, such as would be infirmities that are incompatible with the religious life, a sensible feebleness of mind, untameable passions, a character unable to submit, to obey or to live on good terms with brethren : whoever, I say, fulfils these conditions seems to possess a general fitness for the religious state. The entire lack of one of these essential conditions will be sufficient to lead to the conclusion that the person is not suitable for this state." *

The second sign by which to recognize Divine vocation to the religious state is a decided *attraction* for it. "I give this name," says the above-quoted author, "to that secret voice by which God intimates His will to the soul, and tells it more distinctly the choice He makes for it of such and such a kind of life to which He calls it, or such and such an employment for which He destines it. We understand, by the name of attraction, not only that bias or inclination which seems to forestall all reflexion, and carries on the soul to one kind of life or to one Order rather than to another; but also that deliberate inclination, the fruit of consideration, and of a mature reflection in which, after having weighed the *pro* and the *con*, determines in favour of one side rather than of another. The first attraction is, so to speak, an instinctive one, the second a ⸝rational one: in the first case the heart does almost everything, in the second the impulse has its origin in the intellect, whence it is communicated to the will, and the conviction of the mind determines the persuasion of the heart." †

The description of these two general signs already gives us much light in discerning the will of Heaven in the great business of vocation to the religious

* F. Gautrelet: *Traité de l'Etat Religieux.* vol. i., p. 23., Lyons, 1846.
† The same, p. 25.

state. Still it will be useful to add some special remarks.

In the preceding chapter, when pointing out the persons who were obliged to devote themselves to God by the exercise of the perfect life, we brought out many infallible signs of vocation to the religious life.

The first of these signs is a pressing invitation of grace which, so to say, carries on the will towards the perfect state, and leaves it to enjoy no rest or happiness but in this state.

Next comes a taste, in some degree natural, for the regular life, whose germ has been sown in the soul by grace, and rapidly developed by an innocent life. When this taste is lively and constant, it may be considered as a certain sign of vocation, especially when no outward obstacle hinders this holy inclination. These are vocations of instinct and will which are very evident and very solid.

There are also vocations of reason and conviction: the heart feels a certain repugnance, but the mind sees in the clearest manner that God calls to the perfect life. A Christian may find himself in such a position that whilst on one side he feels a repugnance for the religious life, on the other he is certain that God destines him for it, and that he is obliged to devote himself to it if he wish to be saved. Notwithstanding the resistance of the heart, this conviction ought to carry the day. It manifests the Divine will quite sufficiently. This moral situation is possible, especially with those of the faithful who

join to a piety otherwise solid an unsteady character and ardent passions. In the world these souls
are carried off by the whirl of business and pleasure,
they lose sight entirely of their eternal interests ;
but in the cloister they triumph over their natural
weakness, removed as they are from occasions of
fall and objects of temptation, and they walk on
with great strides in the road of virtue. It is especially souls of this temperament that faithfulness
in answering their vocations decides almost always
their salvation.

We must also consider as particular signs of
vocation to the religious state a great love for one
or another of the advantages of the religious life, or
for one or other of its essential practices.

There are some very high-mettled characters who
distrust themselves, because they feel themselves
capable of acting with much ardour, and are aware
that they are quite incapable of directing themselves. These characters feel an imperative want
of advice, submission and obedience : they do themselves this justice, that, under the management of a
good guide, they think they would be content, feel
at their ease, and be able to fulfil happily all their
duties ; whilst if abandoned to their own counsels
they would go knocking against all kinds of obstacles, just as a ship without a compass, without
sails, rudder or pilot goes dashing against the rocks.
Given up to themselves, these young people will
hurl themselves into a thousand follies, whilst if
they submit to obedience they will feel their sentiments grow greater, their power double, and will

work wonders. Those very souls which could not command themselves will become enlightened guides for others, and will distinguish themselves by their prudence and their energy. I have heard more than one young Christian, full of talent and piety, say, with a full conviction: "To be good I need direction; I can only live under the rule of obedience; I am only at my ease when I obey." These were evidently called to the *religious* life: they entered it and were very happy in it.

Other young people have a decided taste for solitude and retirement. The din of the world, the attraction of pleasures and the joys of earth, which captivate so many hearts, inspire them only with fear and disgust. The quiet of the cloister appears to them perfumed with an all-heavenly peace; outside of it there is for them neither rest nor happiness. In this case, again, the call from Heaven is certain.

There is in certain souls an intense desire to immolate themselves unreservedly to God, and to live absorbed in the thought of His presence and the feeling of His love. God's greatness, majesty, and especially His infinite goodness, make so lively an impression upon them, that they would cast themselves, if they could, into eternity in order to enjoy at once the possession of God, and to be absorbed in Him. For such souls, prevented by extraordinary graces, the world is but a *mirage*, life only a means of arriving speedily at God. Penances, mortifications and austerities, the most painful to nature, count for naught. No sacrifice costs them anything if only it bring them near to God. These vocations have no shadow of a doubt, they are so evidently of God.

It also happens that God calls certain souls to the perfect life by trials and afflictions. Either at one blow, or little by little, He detaches their hearts from all earthly affections; He inspires them with a lively faith and a decided taste for the things of heaven; He shows these souls with a lively and striking clearness the vanity of the world, the shortness of life, and the emptiness of the goods and pleasures of earth; then He gives them to perceive no less forcibly the ineffable happiness of the blessed in heaven. Thus He leads them to esteem and love the religious life. These vocations are pure, holy and certain.

As Divine Providence has a thousand manners of manifesting itself to men, it may suggest or impose the religious vocation by many other signs or tokens, whose meaning will not escape those whom they concern. We have not exhausted the list of the signs of vocation which the Holy Spirit may make use of; and although all of which we have spoken are clear, precise and decisive, we counsel all who meditate upon them or are struck by them, not to come to a definite stop before consulting a good director, who will dispel illusions and serve as a living interpreter of the sensible signs of the Divine will. In so delicate and important a matter we cannot be too prudent, nor keep too scrupulously to the ordinary ways of grace.

CHAPTER XV.

Of the Deliberation Requisite before Embracing the Religious State, and of the Motives that Determine a person to Embrace this State.

OF all states of life that Providence destines for the faithful, the religious state is without doubt that which needs the least deliberation, and the choice of which ought to cause least doubt and to provoke least hesitation. For it is in this state, as we have already observed, that we meet the fewest difficulties and most numerous means of securing our salvation. Thus, when certain doctors, inspired by the maxims of the world rather than by those of the Gospel, pretended, in the times of St. Thomas of Aquin, that nobody could easily make up his mind to embrace the religious state for fear of making a mistake by being unwittingly under the influence of the spirit of darkness, who often transforms himself into an angel of light, so as to make good appear where it is not, the angelic doctor answered that in this matter illusion was so little to be feared that, if the devil *in propria persona* were to advise us to embrace the religious life, we should boldly follow his advice, because he would only be setting before us the advice of our Lord Jesus Christ Himself.

At the same time it is wrong in my idea to exclude systematically all deliberation or examination on this point. Very often it is useful to study and to sound the signs of vocation that we find in and about us. Reflection and maturity of judgment give more weight to the definite resolution, and close the way more surely to after regrets and to turning back. In a resolution of such importance levity, enthusiasm, and over-haste is always harmful. Deliberation opens the mind to the manifestations of God's will, and makes it comprehend and appreciate them all the better.

Over and above the object of the principal resolution there are several other points to be decided. For instance, what manner of life shall I embrace? Am I called to the active or the contemplative life? To works of charity or to the sacred ministry, or to teaching? To which Order should I give the preference? What is the institution for which I have most fitness and for which I feel the greatest attraction? What are the motives which engage me to enter the religious state? Are they pure and supernatural? Have I no more duties to fulfil in the world before enjoying myself in it? Am I perfectly free and disengaged? What steps must I take to separate myself for ever from the world, its ties and its cares? By what resolutions can I render my calling sure, and secure my future? How can I give God evidence of the gratitude I owe Him for the grace of so precious a vocation?

These questions and others suchlike suggested by the position of the person or by circumstances will

be easily and usefully decided in the quiet of a
retreat and with the light of Christian deliberation.
I, therefore, advise all persons who think themselves called to the religious state to recollect
themselves some days before making their definite
resolution, in order to place themselves more
specially under the protection of our Lord, of
the Blessed Virgin and of their holy patrons.
This deliberation is, without doubt, the best
possible preparation for the final decision that
is to fix their lot for life, and, we may say, for
eternity too.

What I have said about the ease with which it is
allowed to embrace the religious state, if a person
have a certain fitness for it and love it, proves how
imprudent, sometimes unjust or even guilty, in
God's eyes, are Christian parents who, through a
worldly spirit or vain attachment, avarice, whim or
obstinacy, refuse their children for whole years
together leave to engage in the religious life. They
fear disappointment and regret; they wish to forestall the chance of a return; preliminary trials
seem necessary; they force their children to appear
much in the world, to enjoy its pleasures and taste
its delights: and these trials sometimes succeed so
far as to stifle a vocation that is really of God, and
at others to affect a healthy constitution by con-
tradiction and disappointment. This conduct of
some parents is neither just, nor Christian, nor
reasonable. They trespass on God's domain,
they substitute the wisdom of the flesh for that of
the Gospel, and often cause the misfortune of their

N

children. I would not say so in such strong terms
were it not that I have often been afflicted with
this sad sight, which ought to be unknown among
Christians. Without doubt, trials are needed
before embracing the perfect life, but the Church
has determined these trials ; it is not in the world,
but in the cloister, that they must be undergone.
The religious orders are more interested than
parents in not receiving subjects who have no
chance of persevering in them. Persons who enter
without vocation cause trouble and disorder, and
even become a source of unhappiness. Be, therefore, content with the reasonable trials that the
Church herself exacts. Do not impose such as act
quite opposite to the end proposed and, at most,
only serve to stifle real vocations.

There is another rock that Christian parents
ought carefully to avoid : it is the imprudent
custom of inducing their children to embrace the
religious life for temporal or fleshly motives—
motives which really do not exist, and which, in
any case, cannot serve to uphold a religious vocation. This artifice was very common formerly,
and is not altogether unknown in our own days.
In order to develope a taste for the religious life in
young souls which they wish to turn towards this
state, they represent the practices and exercises of
monastic life as agreeable to sense, as sweeter, even
according to the world, than the secular life. They
make much of its rest, its indolence, ease, certain
honours, a certain respect, which have their value
with worldly people, but which do not exist or have

no worth in the cloister. Through carelessness
many preachers lose sight of that part of the religious life which is austere and painful to nature,
and picture it to the senses under the most agreeable colours. This is wrong; perhaps a source of
deception. "I declare," says Bourdaloue, "that I
do not like to hear preachers representing the
monastic life to us as a sweet life, exempt from
troubles and disentangled from all care. You
would say, if you heard them, that the religious
has nothing to suffer, nothing to put up with; that
he lacks nothing, that everything is pleasing to
him, that everything turns out according to his
wishes. For one home that he has quitted, a
hundred and more are open to him; for a father or
mother he has parted from, he will have as many
superiors charged with his management. All this
is very nice; but the misfortune is that it is hardly
according to the Gospel. And wherefore should he
renounce the world, if there be there the hundredfold that Jesus Christ hath promised us, and which
one would have to wait for in religion? Besides
the fact that many things will be found to disap-
point the hopes conceived on embracing the religious state, it would also be without doubt
very strange that a person should seek outside
of the world that which they pretend to fly
when they leave the world: that is to say,
purely temporal advantages and altogether natural
sweetnesses.

"The great advantage of the religious profession is Christian self denial, mortification of

sense, the Cross: that is the point of view from which we ought to look at it. All that keeps away from this point of view keeps away from the truth, and consequently is only an illusion. I would not have a young girl (and the same applies to a young man) deceived, who forms the design of retiring into God's house, and feels herself called thither. I would not have anything disguised from her by brilliant but false pictures; let her see all the consequences of the choice she is making; let things be set before her as they are, and let her have pointed out to her the thorns with which the path she is entering is sown. For what in reality is the religious life but the Gospel reduced to practice, and the most perfect practice? And what is the Gospel but the law of renouncing self, of death to self, of perpetual war against self?

"But, you will say to me, these thoughts may discourage a soul and repel it. Well, I answer that, quite the contrary, she can and ought to draw therefrom the most proper motives to make her resolution and confirm herself in it. And why? Because it is from this that she learns to esteem the religious state for that which makes it precisely and supremely worthy of esteem, viz.: As a state of sanctification, of perfection, of salvation; as a state in which the religious soul can every day amass fresh merits for eternity, and incessantly accumulate crowns after crowns: the capital point to which alone she ought to cling, and in which she ought to make all her happiness on earth consist." *

But God has promised the hundredfold, even in this life, to the souls that follow Him in the way of self-denial and the Cross.

"The hundredfold in this life," answers the same pious author, "can only be for a religious soul, the peace she enjoys in her state, and which alone is worth a hundred times as much as all the inheritances and goods which she renounces. . . . But what is this peace ? That is the essential point. . . . When Jesus Christ gave peace to His disciples, He warned them at the same time that it was not a peace, such as the world understands and desires it I give you *My* peace, the Divine Master said to them; it is *Mine*, and not the world's. This peace of the world, this false and condemned peace, is an idle and soft peace, founded on ease and comfort of life, on all that pleases nature and satisfies self-love ; but the peace of the religious soul is established on quite contrary principles—on self-hatred, on a perpetual sacrifice of sensual appetites, inclinations, passions, and will. So that the religious can only be content in his retirement in so far as he knows how to humble himself, crucify himself, overcome himself, and make himself obedient, poor, patient, assiduous in labour, exact in his duties, dispensing himself from

* Bourdaloue : *Pensées*, in his *Works*, vol. xv., p. 114, sq. Besançon, 1823.

nothing, not humouring himself in anything, not wishing to be spared on any point. This will cost him something; but, by a kind of miracle, the less he humours himself, the less he spares himself, the more abundantly he feels peace diffused through his heart.

" And is it not plain, besides, that it is just in the most regular and most austere communities that most satisfaction is evinced, and the yoke of Jesus Christ found to be sweetest and His burden lightest? Everything contributes to this content and quiet of a truly religious soul; the indifference in which she is placed with regard to all things human, and her freedom from all those interests which cause worldlings so much disquiet; entire abandonment of self into the hands of superiors, leaving them to conduct according to their good pleasure and their plans; calm of conscience, the expectation of that sovereign beatitude to which alone she aspires, and to advance towards which by fresh steps she is daily labouring; and, above all, the inward unction of Divine grace which fills her; for God, faithful to His Word, has a thousand secret ways of communicating Himself to this soul, and overwhelming her with the purest delights.

" Judging from the outside, nothing appears at all in this scheme of life, except what is painful and revolting: enclosure, solitude, silence, continual dependence on another, blind submission, a chafing rule, awkward observances, laborious tasks, humiliating exercises, abstinence, fasts, maceration of the flesh. But beneath this outside, so well calculated to terrify souls that have never penetrated deeper, and have learnt by no experience to know the mysteries of God, how many hidden consolations are there not set apart, according to the prophets, for those who fear the Lord ?

"Hence it happens that whilst people in the world, with all their goods, honours and pleasures, are almost always discontented and incessantly grumbling about their lot, the religious in all his nakedness and obscurity, under the most rigid obedience and the most mortifying practices, never ceases blessing his condition and peaceably goes through his career. The peace he possesses is God's peace ; and the Apostle, who had experienced it himself, assures us that God's peace is above all sense, and that nothing in the world is like it.

" This, I repeat, is how I would have the happiness of their state represented to religious persons. This is what I would insist upon, and which will serve to excite their zeal, watchfulness and fervour, by teaching them that they are only happy in this, but that in this they are fully and constantly happy." *

If we would forestall all illusion and all deception, therefore, on the part of aspirants to the religious life, we must beware of boasting of the sweetnesses it offers to sense and the advantages it bestows upon nature. For both sense and nature

* Bourdaloue, as above, p. 118, sq.'

it is at bottom nothing but a sacrifice, a suffering, a mortification; but for the mind it is repose, light and sweet contemplation; and for the heart, love, brotherhood, hope, joy and happiness. Those who engage themselves in it for temporal motives are certain to be unhappy; those who embrace it in a spirit of self-denial, devotion, love of God and of their neighbour, are certain to be happy.

Examples are more eloquent than words; so, to give a just idea of the motives which may determine a young Christian to embrace the religious life, I will here introduce a deliberation written out by a candidate for the cloister at the time when he was examining his vocation. As it contains most of the considerations which occur in such circumstances when a person is guided by the Spirit of God, those who cannot give a full account of their interior will read it with profit. They will find therein a mirror for their soul and an echo of their thoughts, and they will arrive, by way of comparison, at a better understanding of what God demands from them. This deliberation is written in the form of a letter to a director. It runs as follows :—

"Dear Rev. Father,—According to the advice you gave me this morning, during Holy Communion I recommended the affair of my vocation to our Lord Jesus Christ, to the Blessed Virgin, and to my good angel, in order that they might enlighten me and guide me in my choice. I felt the want of their help all the more keenly, because I had been for two years more undecided and blind than ever. Even yesterday, my heart at one time carried me off towards the religious life by an ardent desire of consecrating myself to God ; at another my imagination started as out of sleep and invited me to follow the ways of the world. Still I had never lost the confidence that my good mother had inspired me with towards the Blessed Virgin Mary, and this confidence has always made me hope to see clearly in the matter of my vocation, and to decide with a full knowledge of the case, and with great generosity for the part God should destine me to.

" I must tell you, first of all, dear rev. father, that from my earliest years I have felt in the midst of my heart a great esteem for the religious state, and a desire for the religious life, at first vague and uncertain, afterwards more clearly defined. The first time in my life that I visited a monastery, wherein the austere practices of the religious life were observed in all their rigour, I was deeply impressed by it, although still very young, and I understood that in this manner of life there was something grand and noble which brought one near to God. This impression was never effaced from my heart, and I like to fix my attention upon it as upon one of the sweetest memories of my childhood.

" When I examine in silence and in prayer this inclination, which rises so often in the depths of my heart and analyze my thoughts, I find that I am moved by the purest motives in my desires and my affection for this state.

" What strikes me, especially in the religious

life, is the astonishing ease with which a person
can serve God with all his heart and work His
salvation without fear of great obstacles. The
monastery appears to me like a calm harbour,
where tempests have no entrance, and the gales
of worldly passion can hardly do any damage.
The security in it is great, without the hope of
reward being lessened. On the contrary, God
makes the most brilliant promises to those who
will follow generously in the way of His Cross.

" Contemplating the religious state with the
eyes of faith, I also perceive great honour and
great consolation in it, on account of the resemblance to Jesus Christ, which it produces in all
who embrace it. All Christian perfection consists
in the imitation of our Lord Jesus Christ, and
nowhere do persons imitate Him better or more
constantly than in the religious life. There they
carry His cross and walk in His footsteps towards
Calvary and towards heaven. This thought appears very consoling to me amidst the miseries of
this life.

" The vanity of the world, the shortness of life,
the nearness of death, the uncertainty of salvation,
the length of eternity, and the greatness of the
promised reward are so many more considerations
and motives which urge me to the religious life.
I cannot look without pity upon those thousands
of worldlings who wear themselves out in struggles
and disappointments, in order to hoard a little gold,
some smoke of honour, a few days of pleasure, and
who on the eve of obtaining them, or the day after

they have succeeded, have to go and give an
account to God of their mortal life. This altogether fleshly life appears to me the height of folly,
because it ends in the greatest possible misfortune.
And what, at most, is the longest life compared with
eternity ? And what can I receive in exchange for
my soul ? Ought I not to do everything for its
sake ? If I lose it, all is lost; if I gain it, all is
gained. What good will it be to me to have con-
quered the world if I come to lose my soul? I
wish, therefore, to take the surest side and never
to depart from it. In order to be God's during
eternity, I will apply myself to trying to be His
all my life.

"Moreover, will my sacrifice be great? By
leaving the world do I not also leave behind its
illusions, deceptions, entanglements and miseries?
How many vexations, jealousies and sadnesses are
they not in this world which they call happy? Now
the death of a parent, now the loss of a fortune, at
one time calumny, at another persecution, poison
life—and where one expects to meet nothing but joy
and happiness, nothing, alas! is met but subjects
of tears and misery. Wherefore, then, should we
attach ourselves to this world? Wherefore not
quit it?

" In the monastic life, on the other hand, what
attractions are there not for me ?

" I feel in my heart's midst a very lively senti-
ment of gratitude towards God and of self-devotion to
Him. It seems to me that I should be very happy if
I could offer Him all that I have and all that I am.

" The sacrifice of my goods, fortune, honours and
pleasures is that which will cost me least, because
I know that all these goods, so seducing in appearance, are surrounded with thorns and filled with
bitterness. But I shall be happy to offer to Him
the sacrifice of my parents, brothers and sisters
and friends, whom I shall leave for His sake without loving them the less. This sacrifice will cost
nature much, but it will be sweet, because it will
purify and perfect the affections I bear to those so
dear, and will thus prepare my heart to love God
better.

" I shall also make the sacrifice of my will, the
most precious thing I have, and that will be the
most difficult and most meritorious of all; but I
shall do it with joy, because to serve God is to
reign. I shall thus obtain a heavenly director,
because holy obedience will rule over my whole
person and dispose of all my actions. What a
great advantage is this! What a cause of security
and what a source of peace.

" By renouncing the pleasures of sense, I shall
receive all the means necessary for preserving my
heart pure before God, and of practising in all
its perfection the virtue of chastity, that truly
angelic virtue which I love so much, because it
brings peace, beautifies the soul, and makes it like
to God. The vow of chastity will surround me
with a rampart and preserve me from the attacks
of vice. Thus shall I deserve to be ranked among
the virgins who follow the Lamb, whitheresoever
He goeth.

"I know, too, that the helps to salvation are almost infinitely multiplied in this holy state. To begin with, vocation to the religious life is, without doubt, a sign of the predilection of God's goodness for those who are gifted with it. The saints see in it a sort of second Baptism, a guarantee of pre-destination, a chain binding the soul which is called to heaven. The special rule directs one's actions towards a holy end approved of by the Church; the humble and modest habit that is worn is a Divine livery, and serves as a constant reminder; the example of brethren is an efficacious stimulant; the charity and watchfulness of superiors are a continual support. The love of perfection and a great esteem for the interior life grow there spontaneously. You know that a host of saints, who have worn the same habit and observed the same rule, are reigning in heaven and praying for the welfare of their brethren who are still in this world. More facilities are found in it for exercising charity towards the faithful, aiding the Church in her work of sanctification and working for the glory of God.

"The esteem which the Church evinces for this holy state, the privileges she grants it, the affection she feels and manifests for the religious orders, contribute also to make me esteem and love it and increase in me the desire of having a shar therein.

"Lastly, the graces that God has granted me from my infancy, watching over my innocence, inspiring me with a horror of sin and a love of

virtue, preserving me from a thousand dangers
beneath which I have seen many of the companions
of my early years succumb, appear to make it a
duty for me to consecrate myself to God, in order
to finish by my voluntary co-operation that which
God hath begun in me.   I was received when yet
very young into the Congregation of the Holy
Angels ; I am proud to reckon myself now among
the Children of Mary, and I feel a strong inclination for piety.   Distaste for the religious life only
comes upon me at times when I neglect a little my
duties of piety, when I relax in prayer, or when I
explore the world with vain curiosity.   But as soon
as I return to God, and especially to the day and
hour of Holy Communion, I feel the desire of consecrating myself to the religious life redoubled
within me.

"I have unrolled before you, dear rev. father,
all the folds of my heart.   I have not hidden from
you any of my sentiments, desires, or fears.   I beg
you, then, to examine the motives which induce
me to embrace the religious state, and if you
believe me called by God to this holy state, tell it
me plainly.   This sacrifice will, without doubt,
cost nature much, but it will be very sweet to my
heart.   If God asks it of me, I am ready to offer
it Him."

The above is a detailed and almost perfect ex-
position of the motives which can induce a Christian soul to consecrate herself to God in the
exercise of the perfect life.   Those who make up
their minds for this part, through one or more of

these motives, will certainly find themselves in the good road, and are sure of not making a mistake.

To these indications add fervent prayer and the advice of a good director, and be persuaded that if you will seek for the expression of God's will you will find it.

CHAPTER XVI.

Of Vocation to the Apostleship, or to Missions in Foreign Countries and among Infidels.

THE apostleship which our Lord Jesus Christ established in His lifetime, in order to convert the world to the Christian faith, was not extinguished at the death of the twelve Apostles, who were charged with its inauguration and the exhibition of its prodigious efficacy. The great personal prerogatives, such as universal jurisdiction and infallibility, granted by our Divine Saviour to the twelve Apostles, did, it is true, cease at their death, to live only in the successors of their Prince, St. Peter; but the mission they had received of preaching the Gospel to all the world survived them; and their successors in the pastoral ministry and in the sacred orders have been charged by them to continue it. The bishops succeeded the Apostles in their ministry, and priests came to aid the bishops. St. Clement attests that the Apostles

themselves chose their successors to continue their
mission ; and in fact the apostleship has been continued always through the course of centuries ; and
in every age new peoples have been added to the
Church, and have marshalled themselves beneath
the standard of the Cross.

The mission of the seventy-two Disciples was a
sort of offspring from the apostleship. They pre-
figured the priests sent by bishops to prepare their
ways.

The work of the conversion of pagans and
idolaters is the work of all Christian ages ; it has
never been interrupted ; it continues in our days
with more brilliance and more success than ever.

It is a very remarkable thing that, in the first
years of this century, when there were so many
ruins to restore in Europe, the Church was busying
herself with Catholic missions among infidels, and
that she saw a host of apostles for the heathen rise
in her midst, before she could ordain priests enough
to fill up the ranks of the sacred army in her ancient
churches. At this present day there are in France
hundred of *communes* which once possessed a parish
governed by a rector, and which are now without
priests ; and yet thousands of missionaries go out
every year from Europe for the heathen countries
of Asia, Africa, America and Oceania. Is, then,
this armament opposed to the plans of Providence ? No ; on the contrary, it is an indication
of their tendency. The vocations of these pious
missionaries are from God ; they are very clearly
determined. Were these generous apostles not

to obey the voice that calls them and the power that urges them on, they would think they were disobeying God, and would be altogether miserable. They cry out with the Apostle: "Wo is unto me if I preach not the Gospel!" * It is, therefore, certain that not only does the exterior command given by our Lord Jesus Christ to His Church, of preaching the faith to infidels, yet survive, but, moreover, that the inward voice of our Heavenly Father, which makes the accomplishment of that command possible and easy, is still heard in the midst of men's hearts, and prepares those wonderful vocations of which we are witnesses.

The Catholic apostleship flourishes, then, in the Church, and bears fruit. God's grace chooses out for itself, in the midst of the faithful, the future pillars of the apostleship; the work begun eighteen centuries ago cannot slacken.†

Since we have explained the nature of secular ecclesiastical vocation and of vocation to the religious state, we shall do well to complete this sketch by offering some advice upon the nature

* 1. Cor. ix. 16.

† [The glory of France, amid all her humiliations, is still, as when the pious author wrote, the generousness with which she furnishes apostles in overflowing abundance for the heathen of every part of the world. Since the date of this work—1856—England has made a step towards sharing, at least in part, this glory. The establishment of St. Joseph's Society of Foreign Missions, and the success of its college at Mill Hill, near London, are happy auguries of a rich harvest of apostles: *felix seges.*—TRANS.]

O

and duties of the apostolic vocation, for it also has
particular characters and special duties.

I will not insist upon the greatness of this vocation. It strikes us; ravishes and transports us,
however slightly we consider it. To become an
apostle in the Church is to share, in a particular manner, in the functions of the first twelve
Apostles, and to continue the primitive apostleship.
By preaching to the faithful we are, doubtless,
treading in the footsteps of the Apostles ; but the
conversion of infidels has always been considered
as a work set apart—a work which needs a special
commission of the Church and an extraordinary
grace of God. Often this work has been accom-
panied with miracles and wonders, and that only
not in the first ages, but even in these latter days.

It is, above all, the fruits of this apostleship
which prove the spiritual fecundity of the Church,
and which raise the true spouse of Jesus Christ
above the separated Churches, which are really
adulteresses who have left the domestic roof and
are running in the paths of perdition. The success
of the Catholic apostleship is also one of the
glories of God's people, because it attests the
presence of our Lord Jesus Christ amidst His
own, and His supernatural action upon souls, not
only in the apostles whom He raises up, but also
in the neophytes He makes.

To the apostleship is promised a particular glory
in heaven. "They that instruct many shall shine
as stars for all eternity." * And this is especially

* Dan. xii. 3.

true of apostles, by whose means God shows, for the first time, the wonderful things of His goodness to peoples yet sitting in the shadow of death.

If the vocation of the first twelve Apostles was for them a sign of predilection on the part of our Lord, who said to them, "You have not chosen me, but I have chosen you,"* is it not certain that now also vocation to the apostleship is, on God's part, a particular sign of affection and love for those whom He calls?

This vocation is, therefore, very noble and very precious, whether we consider its end, its origin, or its principle.

In order to enlighten those to whom God grants it, I will briefly mark out three points, viz. :—

I. The motives which a person may and ought to set before himself in embracing this vocation.

II. The qualities of mind, heart, and body with which he ought to be endowed, in order to embrace it with safety.

III. The precautions he ought to take to answer it successfully.

I. Of the principal motives necessary to follow the apostolic vocation.

In order for a person to see whether he be truly called of God to the Catholic apostleship among heretics or infidels, it is enough for him to examine what are the motives that engage him to embrace this career, and what are the dispositions that he

---

* John xv. 16.

brings to this holy state; for these motives and dispositions are really the undoubted signs of God's will in us.

We may be sure, to begin with, that God does not call to the apostolic functions those who wish to devote themselves to it for temporal motives or fickle reasons. So, for instance, if a person wished to give himself to the missions out of a spirit of curiosity and adventure, in order to see far-off countries and to become acquainted with the manners and customs of little-known peoples, or through a love of novelty and change, or to satisfy a species of inclination for extraordinary enterprizes, or through vanity in getting himself talked about, or to distinguish himself from others; in these cases we cannot reasonably believe that God gives rise to such desires, or approves of such projects. We must attribute to them, as their first cause, great fickleness of character, a more or less romantic spirit, and perhaps also a great natural inconstancy. Now, these are not sentiments or dispositions which can serve as a basis for a Divine vocation.

If a person determined to embrace the apostleship, through vexation or disgust, on account of some displeasure caused him by superiors, or of a painful quarrel with his equals, he ought to distrust such whims, and submit them, first of all, to a strong trial; for such circumstances, even though they may become the occasion of a real vocation, still can never be its motive.

We should also distrust very particularly vocations that are too sudden and too ardent to come from the Holy Spirit; for the Holy Spirit acts always with due weight and measure, and is never to be found in bustle and noise. If a person wishes to throw himself all at once into missionary life without any preparation; if he is excited, if he is ready to break down everything in order to arrive at once at his end, if he chafes at the obstacles which hinder the fulfilment of his project, or at persons who oppose it, we may be sure that these motives and desires come not from God, but from the flesh, and that he ought not to dwell upon them.

In order to follow surely and confidently the career of the apostleship, we must devote ourselves to it out of supernatural, solid and deliberate motives, which are the only ones that God is wont to suggest to those souls whom He calls to a great and noble mission.

The three principal motives that we may set before us to embrace the apostolic career are:—

Firstly, a great desire of working for God's glory;

Nextly, an ardent zeal for the welfare of souls;

Thirdly, a holy ambition to imitate the Apostles, and to share in their labours, merits, and rewards.

When a man is animated by these three sentiments, and superiors consent, he may believe himself called of God to the apostolic career.

The first sign of vocation is a great desire of working for God's glory. This desire is easily recognized. Every day we express it in the Lord's Prayer, when we ask God that His name may be hallowed among men, and that His kingdom may come. But in order that this desire may rise to the rank of a sign of Divine vocation to the apostleship, it must produce in the soul a profound and studied esteem of the glory of God, the immortal King of Ages, and an ardent need must be felt of contributing to it with all one's strength and power. When a person sets before him the conversion of infidels or the bringing back of heretics into unity, in order to people the Holy Sion, to increase the number of the inhabitants of the Heavenly Jerusalem, to replace the angels who have fallen from their thrones into the depths of hell, to add new ornaments to the court of the King of Glory, and to fill up the number of the elect : then such a person is truly animated with zeal for God's glory, and is obeying the inspirations of His grace. Such a sentiment can come only from God, and is certainly of such a nature as to keep up in the soul the apostolic spirit and vocation to the apostleship.

Again, it is this same zeal for God's glory that animates that soul, which in its labours proposes to itself the exaltation of Holy Mother Church, and the daily spreading of the kingdom of Jesus Christ upon earth. The triumphs of His Spouse over hell, the filling up of what is wanting of His Passion, according to the expression of the Apostle, accomplished by the propagation of the faith and the

application of the sacraments; all these again are
things which contribute directly to God's glory
and show it forth amid the peoples, works in which
no one can aspire to co-operate, unless he be
animated with a truly apostolical spirit, with the
zeal that makes apostles.

Why has the Society of Jesus produced so large
a number of apostolical men in so few years?
Because St. Ignatius animated his disciples with
that zeal for God's glory which consumed himself
and which caused him to adopt as the word of
command, and the great motive of all actions, that
beautiful and noble maxim : " All for God's greater
glory ! "

This motive is the first and noblest that can
be proposed in the exercise of Christian virtue :
it is also the most necessary for the apostles,
whose mission it is to propagate this glory. Without doubt we must all work for it, since there
is disorder wherever God is not glorified ; but
apostles are obliged to have it incessantly before
their eyes, and to aim at it constantly, not only
by the practice of the works of ordinary life, but
often also by the exercise of heroic virtues, such as
that of martyrdom.

Zeal for God's glory, when carried to a high
degree, is thus a certain sign of Divine vocation
to the apostleship.

Zeal for the salvation of souls, when lively and
ardent, has the same significance. Real apostles
are penetrated with a sentiment of profound com-
passion for so many millions of souls which have

the misfortune to be lost, because they know not our Lord Jesus Christ, and are deprived of the grace by aid of which they might be saved. They behold the vast harvest that our Lord shows us in the Gospel, a harvest already yellow and ripe, calling for the hand of the reapers: and, seeing it partly abandoned, they burn with the desire of putting their hands to it, and gathering it into the granary of the Goodman of the house. As Abraham, when returning home, they say, but in another sense, and say constantly: "Give me the souls, and the rest take to thyself."* The fate of these unhappy infidels touches them, penetrates them with pity, and inspires them with an ardent charity, capable of all sacrifice and devotion. Especially when they learn that tribes, still heathen, are calling aloud for the black robes, the ministers of the Great Spirit, to teach them "the good prayer,"—for such is their language,—these true apostles feel transported with zeal, and have no more rest until they are consecrated to this great work of the conversion of the heathen. When they hear that peoples are tarrying with a certain good faith in the heresy that has been bequeathed to them by their fathers, and yet oppose no resistance to the truth, they feel led to brave all obstacles, in order to offer to these poor people the torch of faith, and to bring them back to the fold of the Good Shepherd.

This zeal for the salvation of souls may become

* Gen. xiv. 21.

so ardent that they cry out from the bottom of their heart with the Apostle : " I wish myself to be an anathema for my brethren,"* and to sacrifice myself for their sake. Were I to sacrifice my health or my life, I still wish to save these souls and lead them into heaven. No sacrifice will cost me anything, provided that Jesus Christ be preached to all that know Him not, and loved by those who have abandoned Him.

Such were the heroic sentiments that animated the great Apostle of the Indies, St. Francis Xavier, and inspired him with his beautiful prayer for the conversion of infidels—a prayer which fervent Christians ought to recite daily, and which the apostles of God ought to have constantly on their lips.

Whoever feels in the depths of his heart this zeal for the welfare of souls, and this ardent desire of contributing to the conversion of infidels and the sanctification of sinners, is called of God to the Catholic apostleship, and may apply himself thereto with entire confidence.

Lastly, there is a third motive which is from heaven : I mean a holy ambition of imitating our Lord Jesus Christ and the Apostles in their apostolic labours, of treading in their footsteps by the preaching of the Gospel, of continuing their work, of sharing their toils, their sufferings, their merits, their glory and their crown. The twelve special thrones which God has prepared in heaven for His

* Rom. ix. 3.

first twelve Apostles will also be possessed by the apostolic men who have succeeded them, and who have followed the course of their triumphs. The ambition of following them here below, in order to enjoy with them in heaven the crown of the apostleship, comes from God, and is a natural result of apostolic vocation. It is a support in labours ; it ever becomes, when nourished by faith and charity, the principle of great undertakings, great self-devotion and great success. He who is quickened by it may give himself up to the toils of the apostleship with the sweet confidence that he will be upheld by the hands of the Apostles whom he is imitating and by our Lord Himself, who is the Chief and the Soul of the Apostles.

I have now described the character which is stamped on those souls whom God calls to the labours of the Catholic apostleship. Let every one, before throwing himself into this noble and holy career, examine whether he can perceive in himself the Divine seal of vocation.

II. Of the qualities and habits needed for the apostleship in those who are truly called thereunto.

Here, as elsewhere, the first sign of Divine vocation to a particular state is, without doubt, fitness to fulfil its duties. Let us, therefore, inquire what are the qualities essentially needed in an apostle of the Gospel ?

He needs, first of all, certain qualities of *mind*. In the first place I would rank the spirit of faith. In order to preach the truth to unbelievers, he

must be thoroughly penetrated with it himself.
He who has a lively and ardent faith easily communicates his belief, because it gushes forth at one
and the same time from his mind, from his mouth
and from his heart; he has so drunk it in, he is so
penetrated with it himself, he can explain its
sublime beauties to philosophers, and communicate
its sweet and simple lights to the blindest minds.
In teaching the faith he easily seizes that side
which may strike those whom he is addressing : he
can make his teaching loftier or simpler, according
to the needs of his audience.   Without this lively
spirit of faith a missionary cannot succeed ; if he
be poor he will have nothing to give.   A languid
or spiritless teaching will produce no conviction, and
remains necessarily barren.   The Catholic apostle
needs, therefore, a great spirit of faith, fed by
prayer, meditation and study.

Although God does not always require profound
learning in those whom He chooses as instruments
of His mercies, still He would not have them reckon
on miraculous inspirations in order to preach the
faith ; He requires that they employ the ordinary
means of obtaining that sacred science which they
need to instruct others easily.   They who have a
scarce passable knowledge, and who do not apply
themselves to complete it by study, show slight dispositions for becoming doctors in Israel, and little
fitness for treading in the footsteps of the Apostles.

Nor do I think that young men who are by
nature giddy, fickle or inconstant, who allow themselves to be greatly moved by the attractions of

novelty, and who follow the impulses of their
imagination much more willingly than the oracles
of reason, can be called to the apostleship.   An
apostle of Jesus Christ needs much calmness, much
maturity of mind, and, moreover, a very sound
judgment.   He needs a certain concentration,
which secures for him the full use of his strength,
and a tranquillity which allows him ever to with-
stand error and to forestall the sudden attacks of
false science.   This seriousness of spirit, which the
interior life always confers, is an essential quality
for a true apostle.   He who has not yet acquired
it, at least to a certain extent, has reason to doubt
of his vocation to the apostolic life.

An apostle of God also needs eminent qualities of
heart, especially that charity of which we have
spoken above, consisting in the perfect love of God
and our neighbour.   This charity, when highly
developed, explicit, active and ardent, is the very
soul and life of the missioner.   It is this which
rules his whole conduct and person, which raises
him to that supernatural order whence he gathers
all his strength.   Through the effect of this twofold love he becomes sincerely humble, submissive
of heart to God and his lawful superiors, obedient
as a child, gentle as a lamb.   From this spirit of
charity springs up in his heart the spirit of sacrifice
and self-devotion, self-denial, patience in all trials,
and a zeal which nothing can cool or tire.

But this is not all.   He needs also habits of
virtue, and, above all, the habit of prayer and union
with God.   Constancy in the practice of the exer-

cises of ordinary piety, great assiduousness in fre-
quenting the sacraments, mortification of sense,
the modesty befitting a priest and victory over passions, are, without doubt, conditions requisite as a
preparation for the apostolic life. This life needs
very solid virtue and a sincere love of good. Laxity
or coldness in the exercise of piety are justly
reckoned as signs of non-vocation to this state. If
St. Paul did not wish the Church to admit neophytes in the faith to Holy Orders,* just so the
Church does not wish neophytes in virtue to be
admitted to the apostleship. This ministry needs
formed and steadfast men, soldiers ready to combat
evil and error in every shape.

It is well known that an apostle of Jesus Christ
must love the Church of God, his spiritual mother,
with a tender love, and profess a sincere attachment to the Sovereign Pontiff, who alone in the
midst of the Christian people has preserved all the
prerogatives of the primitive apostleship.

Lastly, the desire of martyrdom is also one of
the inspirations of the apostolic spirit, and may
become the infallible mark of a true vocation to the
apostleship.

The qualities of *body* requisite for an apostle of
Jesus Christ may be reduced to robust health and
strength sufficient to bear the privations and
fatigues of this laborious life. To give himself
easily to the labours of the apostleship, a man needs
a certain amount of vigour and much courage.

* 1 Tim. iii. 6.

Persons who are weak, sickly, very sensitive to privations, to severity of climate, to changes of temperature, can hardly flatter themselves upon possessing qualities of body necessary for an apostle, nor, consequently, upon being called to the labours of the apostolic life. For the rest, it lies with superiors to judge of the exceptions to which this rule may be liable.

III. Of the precautions to be observed in answering the apostolic vocation.

If you would never make a mistake, the Holy Spirit bids you to do nothing without counsel.*

The first thing to do when preparing for the apostolic life is to fortify oneself with counsels. We should first of all consult God, the Father of Lights, the Holy Spirit, the Divine Source of the gift of counsel. We should also have recourse to the advice of superiors, to our director ; and, lastly, we should search our own heart, in order to be sure of finding in ourselves and about us all that is necessary to form and to uphold a real apostle of Jesus Christ. The idea we have given of the greatness of the undertaking enables us also to grasp the importance of the resolution we have to take, when deliberating on this vocation. It would be the height of rashness not to proceed in this matter with slowness, prudence, and full preparation.

In vain should we hope for the lights of Heaven, if we deserved them not by an upright and pure

---

* Ecclus. xxxii. 24.

intention, fervent prayers and the exercise of a generous penance.

The practice of solid virtues, especially of humility and mortification, is a natural and necessary preparation for the Catholic apostleship. He who would bring back peoples to God, and attach them to Him for life, must begin by living himself in the strictest union with God. Let him prelude the labours of the apostleship by the exercise of good works, as far as his actual position will permit. If he is already engaged in the priesthood, let him fashion himself for his future labours by undertakings of zeal and a perfect practice of the functions of the sacred ministry.

All other things being equal, it is preferable for all young men who intend themselves for the apostleship to enter a religious order, or to join a religious congregation consecrated to the work of the missions, in order to obtain therein more certain direction and more powerful support. Nobody can fail to recognize the advantage to be obtained from the advice and experience of the superiors of these congregations, all of whose members materally aid and uphold one another. The rule of life the community practises, and the ease of remoulding one's temperament, forestall many dangers and procure many helps and advantages to which isolated missioners can never hope to attain.

Nowadays the congregations and religious orders in which the work of the missions has most developed are numerous enough for choice to be made among them, and for consulting in this important matter even one's personal tastes. The very existence of these corporations in our days proves that, in the Church's mind, the apostleship, to be truly useful to those who exercise it, and really more efficacious in its results, should be exercised by bodies and with common efforts. At the same time a person may also engage himself under the directions of bishops or vicars apostolic, who exercise a fatherly watchfulness over their dear fellow-workers, and aid and uphold them by that feeling of heroic charity who animates them ever and everywhere.

Let, then, souls called of God to the sublime vocation of the apostleship measure the greatness of this heavenly favour, and the importance of the duties it imposes. But as soon as they are convinced of the intentions of God's will in their regard, let them listen no longer to flesh and blood, but march courageously on, looking neither to right nor to left, crying from their hearts' depths : " *God wills it! God wills it!*"

THE END.

Printed by D. Lane, 310, Strand, London, W.C.

A Select Catalogue of Books

PUBLISHED BY

BURNS, OATES, & CO.,

17 & 18, PORTMAN STREET,

AND

63, PATERNOSTER ROW.

BOOKS LATELY PUBLISHED

BURNS, OATES, & CO.,

17 & 18, Portman Street, and 63, Paternoster Row.

———◦◇◦———

Memorials of those who Suffered for the Faith in Ireland in the Sixteenth, Seventeenth, and Eighteenth Centuries. Collected from Authentic and Original Documents by MYLES O'REILLY, B.A., LL.D. 8vo, 7s. 6d.

"A very valuable compendium of the martyrology of Ireland during the three, or rather two, centuries of active Protestant persecution. The language of many of these original records, written often by a friend or relative of the martyr, is inexpressibly touching, often quite heroic in its tone."—*Dublin Review.*

"Very interesting memories."—*Month.*

———

Life of St. Thomas of Canterbury. By Mrs. HOPE, Author of "The Early Martyrs" Cloth extra, 4s. 6d.

A valuable addition to the collection of historical books for Catholic readers. It contains a large collection of interesting facts, gleaned with great

BURNS, OATES, & CO., 17, PORTMAN STREET, W.

industry from the various existing Lives of St. Thomas, and other documents.

"Compiled with great care from the best authors."—*Month.*

"The rich covers of this splendidly-bound volume do not, as is often the case, envelop matter unworthy of its fair exterior. This is a volume which will be found useful as a present, whether in the college or school, for either sex."—*Weekly Register.*

"An agreeable and useful volume."—*Nation.*

"A more complete collection of incidents and anecdotes, combined with events of greater weight, could not be compressed into so compact, yet perfectly roomy, a space."—*Tablet.*

By the same Author.

Life of St. Philip Neri. New Edition.
2s. 6d. ; cheap edition, 2s.

NARRATIVE OF MISSIONS.

The Corean Martyrs. By Canon SHORTLAND. Cloth, 2s.

A narrative of Missions and Martyrdoms too little known in this country.

"This is a notice of the martyrs who have fallen in this most interesting mission, and of the history of its rise and progress up to the present day."—*Tablet.*

"No one can read this interesting volume without the most genuine admiration of, and sympathy with, such zeal and constancy."—*Literary Churchman.*

MISSIONARY BIOGRAPHY.

1. Life of Henri Dorié, Martyr. Translated by Lady HERBERT. 1s. 6d. ; cloth, 2s.

"The circulation of such lives as this of Henry Dorie will do much to promote a spirit of zeal, and to move hearts hitherto stagnant because they have not been stirred to the generous deeds which characterise Catholic virtues."—*Tablet*.

2. *Théophane Vénard, Martyr in Tonquin.*
Edited by the Same.   2s. ; cloth elegant, 3s.

" The life of this martyr is not so much a biography as a series of letters translated by Lady Herbert, in which the life of Théophane Vénard unfolds itself by degrees, and in the most natural and interesting way.   His disposition was affectionate, and formed for ardent friendship ; hence, his correspondence is full of warmth and tenderness, and his love of his sister in particular is exemplary and striking.   During ten years he laboured under Mgr. Retord, in the western district of Tonquin, and his efforts for the conversion of souls were crowned with singular success.   During the episcopate of his Bishop no less than 40,000 souls were added to the flock of Christ, and Vénard was peculiarly instrumental in gathering in this harvest." — *Northern Press*.

" We cannot take leave of this little volume without an acknowledgment to Lady Herbert for the excellent English dress in which she has presented it to the British public ; certainly, no lives are more calculated to inspire vocation to the noble work of the apostolic life than those of Dorie and Vénard."—*Tablet*.

3. *Life of Bishop Bruté.*   Edited by the Same.

———

The Martyrdom of St. Cecilia: a Drama.
By ALBANY J. CHRISTIE, S.J.   With a Frontispiece after Molitor.   Elegant cloth, 5s.

" Well-known and beautiful drama."—*Tablet*.

" The receipt of the fourth edition of this beautiful play assures us that our own opinion of its merits has been shared by a wide circle of the Catholic public.   The binding is exquisite, and the picture of St. Cecilia is a work of art."—*Weekly Register*

The Life of M. Olier, Founder of the Seminary of St. Sulpice; with Notices of his most Eminent Contemporaries. By EDWARD HEALY THOMPSON, M.A. Cloth, 4s.

This Biography has received the special approbation of the Abbé Faillon, Author of " La Vie de M. Olier;" and of the Very Reverend Paul Dubreul, D.D., Superior of the Seminary of St. Sulpice, Baltimore, U.S.

Edited by the Same.

The Life of St. Charles Borromeo. Cloth, 3s. 6d.

Also, lately published, by Mr. THOMPSON.

The Hidden Life of Jesus: a Lesson and Model to Christians. Translated from the French of BOUDON. Cloth, 3s.

" This profound and valuable work has been very carefully and ably translated by Mr. Thompson. We shall be glad to receive more of that gentleman's publications, for good translation, whether from the French or any other language, is not too common amongst us. The publication is got up with the taste always displayed by the firm of Burns, Oates, and Co."—*Register.*

" The more we have of such works as ' The Hidden Life of Jesus,' the better."—*Westminster Gazette.*

" A book of searching power."—*Church Review.*

"We have often regretted that this writer's works are not better known."—*Universe.*

" We earnestly recommend its study and practice to all readers." —*Tablet.*

" We have to thank Mr. Thompson for this translation of a valuable work which has long been popular in France."—*Dublin Review.*

" A good translation."—*Month.*

BURNS, OATES, & CO., 63, PATERNOSTER ROW, E.C.

Devotion to the Nine Choirs of Holy Angels,
and especially to the Angel Guardians. Translated from the Same.   3s.

" We congratulate Mr. Thompson on the way in which he has accomplished his task, and we earnestly hope that an increased devotion to the Holy Angels may be the reward of his labour of love."—*Tablet.*

" A beautiful translation."—*The Month.*

" The translation is extremely well done."—*Weekly Register.*

Library of Religious Biography.   Edited by EDWARD HEALY THOMPSON.

Vol. 1.   THE LIFE OF ST. ALOYSIUS GONZAGA, S.J.   5s.

" We gladly hail the first instalment of Mr. Healy Thompson's Library of Religious Biography. The life before us brings out strongly a characteristic of the Saint which is, perhaps, little appreciated by many who have been attracted to him chiefly by the purity and early holiness which have made him the chosen patron of the young. This characteristic is his intense energy of will, which reminds us of another Saint, of a very different vocation and destiny, whom he is said to have resembled also in personal appearance—the great St. Charles Borromeo."—*Dublin Review.*

" The book before us contains numberless traces of a thoughtful and tender devotion to the Saint. It shows a loving penetration into his spirit, and an appreciation of the secret motives of his action, which can only be the result of a deeply affectionate study of his life and character."—*Month.*

Vol. 2.   THE LIFE OF MARIE EUSTELLE HARPAIN ; or, the Angel of the Eucharist.   5s.

" The life of Marie Eustelle Harpain possesses a special value and interest apart from its extraordinary natural and supernatural beauty, from the fact that to her example and to the effect of her writings is attributed in great measure the wonderful revival of devotion to the Blessed Sacrament in France, and consequently throughout Western Christendom."—*Dublin Review.*

" A more complete instance of that life of purity and close union with God in the world of which we have just been speaking is to be found in the history of Marie Eustelle Harpain, the sempstress of Saint-Pallais. The writer of the present volume has had the advantage of very copious materials in the French works on which his own work is founded, and Mr. Thompson has discharged his office as editor with his usual diligence and accuracy."—*The Month.*

Vol. 3. THE LIFE OF ST. STANISLAS KOSTKA. 5s.

" We strongly recommend this biography to our readers, earnestly hoping that the writer's object may thereby be attained in an increase of affectionate veneration for one of whom Urban VIII. exclaimed that, although 'a little youth,' he was indeed 'a great saint.' "—*Tablet.*

"There has been no adequate biography of St. Stanislas. In rectifying this want, Mr. Thompson has earned a title to the gratitude of English-speaking Catholics. The engaging Saint of Poland will now be better known among us, and we need not fear that, better known, he will not be better loved."—*Weekly Register.*

The Life of S. Teresa, written by herself: a new Translation from the last Spanish Edition. To which is added for the first time in English THE RELATIONS, or the Manifestations of her Spiritual State which the Saint submitted to her Confessors. Translated by DAVID LEWIS. In a handsome volume, 8vo, cloth, 10s. 6d.

" The work is incomparable; and Mr. Lewis's rare faithfulness and felicity as a translator are known so well, that no word of ours can be necessary to make the volume eagerly looked for."—*Dublin Review.*

" We have in this grand book perhaps the most copious spiritual autobiography of a Saint, and of a highly-favoured Saint, as exists."—*Month.*

The Life of Margaret Mary Alacoque. By the Rev. F. TICKELL, S.J. 8vo, cloth, 7s. 6d.

" It is long since we have had such a pleasure as the reading of Father Tickell's book has afforded us. No incident of her holy life from birth to death seems to be wanting, and the volume appropriately closes with an account of her beatification."—*Weekly Register.*

"It is one of those high-class spiritual biographies which will be best appreciated in religious communities." — *Westminster Gazette.*

"Of Father Tickell's labours we can say with pleasure that he has given us a real biography, in which the Saint is everything, and the biographer keeps in the background."—*Dublin Review.*

"We can only hope that the life may carry on, as it is worthy of doing, the apostolate begun in our country by one who our Lord desires should be 'as a brother to His servant, sharing equally in these spiritual goods, united with her to His own Heart for ever.'"—*Tablet.*

"The work could hardly have been done in a more unpretending, and at the same time more satisfactory, manner than in the volume now before us."—*Month.*

The Day Hours of the Church.   Latin and English.   Cloth, 1s.

Also, separately,

THE OFFICES OF PRIME AND COMPLINE.   8d.

THE OFFICES OF TIERCE, SEXT, AND NONE.   3d.

"Prime and Compline are the morning and evening prayers which the Church has drawn up for her children; and, for our part, we can wish for nothing better. We know not where an improvement could be suggested, and therefore we see not why anything should have been substituted for them. . . . Why should not their use be restored? Why should they not become the standard devotions of all Catholics, whether alone or in their families? Why may we not hope to have them more solemnly performed—chanted even every day in all religious communities; or, where there is a sufficient number of persons, even in family chapels?"—*Cardinal Wiseman.*

"These beautiful little books, which have received the imprimatur of his Grace the Archbishop, are a zealous priest's answers to the most eminent Cardinal's questions—such answers as would have gladdened his heart could they have been given when first demanded. But the Cardinal lives in his successors and what he so greatly desired should be done is in progress of full performance."—*Tablet.*

"The publication of these Offices is another proof of what we have before alluded to, viz., the increased liturgical taste of the present day."—*Catholic Opinion*

POPULAR DEVOTION.
Now ready.

Devotions for the Ecclesiastical Seasons, consisting of Psalms, Hymns, Prayers, &c., suited for Evening Services, and arranged for Singing. Cloth, 1s. Also in separate Nos. at 2d. each, for distribution, as follows:—

1. Advent and Christmas.
2. Septuagesima to Easter.
3. Paschal Time.
4. Whitsuntide.
5. Sundays after Pentecost.
6. Feasts of our Lady.

7. Saints' Days.

Music for the whole, 1s. 6d.

"A valuable addition to our stock of popular devotions."—*Dublin Review.*

Church Music and Church Choirs: 1. The Music to be Sung; 2. The proper Singers; 3. The Place for the Choir. 2s.

"The special value of this pamphlet, and the seasonableness of its circulation, lie in this: that it attempts to solve—and, we believe, does really solve—several important points as to the proper kinds of music to be used in our public Offices, and more especially at High Mass."—*Tablet.*

"We earnestly recommend all who can do so to procure and study this pamphlet."—*Weekly Register.*

"Masterly and exhaustive articles."—*Catholic Opinion.*

BURNS, OATES, & CO, 63, PATERNOSTER ROW, E.C.

Liturgical Directions for Organists, Singers,
and Composers.   Contains the Instructions of the
Holy See on the proper kind of Music for the
Church, from the Council of Trent to the present
time ; and thus furnishes choirs with a guide for
selection.   Fcp. 8vo, 6d.

New Meditations for each Day in the Year
on the Life of our Lord Jesus Christ.   By a
Father of the Society of Jesus.   With the imprimatur of his Grace the Archbishop of Westminster.   Second Edition.   Vols. I. and II.,
price 4s. 6d. each ; or complete in two vols., 9s.

" We can heartily recommend this book for its style and sub-
stance ; it bears with it several strong recommendations. . . .
It is solid and practical without being dreary or commonplace."
Westminster Gazette.

" A work of great practical utility, and we give it our earnest
recommendation."—*Weekly Register.*

The Day Sanctified : being Meditations and
Spiritual Readings for Daily Use.   Selected from
the Works of Saints and approved writers of the
Catholic Church.   Fcp., cloth, 3s. 6d. ; red
edges, 4s.

" Of the many volumes of meditation on sacred subjects which
have appeared in the last few years, none has seemed to us so well
adapted to its object as the one before us."—*Tablet.*

" Deserves to be specially mentioned."—*Month.*

" Admirable in every sense."—*Church Times.*

" Many of the Meditations are of great beauty. . . . They
form, in fact, excellent little sermons, and we have no doubt will
be largely used as such."—*Literary Churchman.*

Our Father: Popular Discourses on the Lord's Prayer. By Dr. EMANUEL VEITH, Preacher in Ordinary in the Cathedral of Vienna. (Dr. V. is one of the most eminent preachers on the Continent.) Cloth, 3s. 6d.

" We can heartily recommend these as accurate, devotional, and practical."—*Westminster Gazette.*

" We are happy to receive and look over once more this beautiful work on the Lord's Prayer—most profitable reading."—*Weekly Register.*

" Most excellent manual."—*Church Review.*

Little Book of the Love of God. By Count STOLBERG. With Life of the Author. Cloth, 2s.

" An admirable little treatise, perfectly adapted to our language and modes of thought."—*Bishop of Birmingham.*

NEW BOOK FOR HOLY COMMUNION.

Reflections and Prayers for Holy Communion. Translated from the French. Uniform with " Imitation of the Sacred Heart." With Preface by Archbishop MANNING. Fcp. 8vo, cloth, 4s. 6d.; bound, red edges, 5s.; calf, 8s. 6d.; morocco, 9s. 6d.

" The Archbishop has marked his approval of the work by writing a preface for it, and describes it as 'a valuable addition to our books of devotion.' We may mention that it contains ' two very beautiful methods of hearing Mass,' to use the words of the Archbishop in the Preface."—*Register.*

" A book rich with the choicest and most profound Catholic devotions."—*Church Review.*

BURNS, OATES, & CO., 63, *PATERNOSTER ROW, E.C.*

Holy Confidence. By Father ROGACCI, of the Society of Jesus. One vol. 18mo, cloth, 2s.

"As an attack on the great enemy, despair, no work could be more effective; while it adds another to a stock of books of devotion which is likely to be much prized."—*Weekly Register.*

"This little book, addressed to those 'who strive to draw nearer to God and to unite themselves more closely with Him,' is one of the most useful and comforting that we have read for a long time. We earnestly commend this little book to all troubled souls, feeling sure that they will find in it abundant cause for joy and consolation."—*Tablet.*

The Invitation Heeded: Reasons for a Return to Catholic Unity. By JAMES KENT STONE, late President of Kenyon College, Gambier, Ohio, and of Hobart College. Cloth, 5s. 6d.

"A very important contribution to our polemical literature, which can hardly fail to be a standard work on the Anglican controversy."—*Dr. Brownson in the New York Tablet.*

₊ Of this able work 3000 have already been sold in America.

The New Testament Narrative, in the Words of the Sacred Writers. With Notes, Chronological Tables, and Maps. A book for those who, as a matter of education or of devotion, wish to be thoroughly well acquainted with the Life of our Lord. What is narrated by each of His Evangelists is woven into a continuous and chronological narrative. Thus the study of the Gospels is complete and yet easy. Cloth, 2s.

"The compilers deserve great praise for the manner in which they have performed their task. We commend this little volume as well and carefully printed, and as furnishing its readers, more-

over, with a great amount of useful information in the tables inserted at the end."—*Month.*

"It is at once clear, complete, and beautiful."—*Catholic Opinion.*

Balmez: Protestantism and Catholicism
compared in their Effects upon European Civilisa-
tion. Cloth, 7s. 6d.

₊ A new edition of this far-famed Treatise.

The See of St. Peter. By T. W. ALLIES.
A new and improved edition, with Preface on
the present State of the Controversy. 4s. 6d.

Lallemant's Doctrine of the Spiritual Life.
Edited by Dr. FABER. New Edition. Cloth,
4s. 6d.

"This excellent work has a twofold value, being both a biography and a volume of meditations. Father Lallemant's life
does not abound with events, but its interest lies chiefly in the
fact that his world and his warfare were within. His 'Spiritual
Doctrine' contains an elaborate analysis of the wants, dangers,
trials, and aspirations of the inner man, and supplies to the
thoughtful and devout reader the most valuable instructions for
the attainment of heavenly wisdom, grace, and strength."—
Catholic Times.

"A treatise of the very highest value."—*Month.*

"The treatise is preceded by a short account of the writer's
life, and has had the wonderful advantage of being edited by the
late Father Faber."—*Weekly Register.*

"One of the very best of Messrs. Burns and Co.'s publications
is this new edition of F. Lallemant's 'Spiritual Doctrine.'"—
Westminster Gazette.

BURNS, OATES, & CO., 63, PATERNOSTER ROW, E.C.

The Rivers of Damascus and Jordan : a
Causerie. By a Tertiary of the Order of St. Dominick. 4s.

"Good solid reading."—*Month.*

"Well done, and in a truly charitable spirit."—*Catholic Opinion.*

"It treats the subject in so novel and forcible a light, that we are fascinated in spite of ourselves, and irresistibly led on to follow its arguments and rejoice at its conclusions."—*Tablet.*

Eudoxia : a Tale of the Fifth Century.
From the German of IDA, COUNTESS HAHN-HAHN. Cloth elegant, 4s.

"This charming tale may be classed among such instructive as well as entertaining works as 'Fabiola' and 'Callista.' It adds another laurel to the brow of the fair Countess."—*Weekly Register.*

"Instructive and interesting book."—*Northern Press.*

Tales for the Many. By CYRIL AUSTIN.
In Five Numbers, at 2d. each; also, cloth, 1s.; gilt edges, 1s. 6d.

"Calculated to do good in our lending-libraries."—*Tablet.*

"We wish the volume all the success it deserves, and shall always welcome with pleasure any effort from the same quarter."—*Weekly Register.*

"One of the most delightful books which Messrs. Burns and Oates have brought out to charm children at this festive season."—*Catholic Opinion.*

In the Snow; or, Tales of Mount St.
Bernard. By the Rev Dr. ANDERDON. Cloth neat, 3s. 6d.

"A collection of pretty stories."—*Star.*

"An excellent book for a present."—*Universe.*

BURNS, OATES, & CO., 17, PORTMAN STREET, W.

"A capital book of stories."—*Catholic Opinion.*

"An agreeable book."—*Church Review.*

"An admirable fireside companion."—*Nation.*

"A very interesting volume of tales."—*Freeman.*

"Several successive stories are related by different people assembled together, and thus a greater scope is given for variety, not only of the matter, but also the tone of each story, according to the temper and position of the narrators. Beautifully printed, tastefully bound, and reflects great credit on the publishers."

"A pleasing contribution."—*Month.*

"A charming volume. We congratulate Catholic parents and children on the appearance of a book which may be given by the former with advantage, and read by the latter with pleasure and edification."—*Dublin Review.*

By the same Author.

The Seven Ages of Clarewell: A History of a Spot of Ground. Cloth, 3s.

"We have an attractive work from the pen of an author who knows how to combine a pleasing and lively style with the promotion of the highest principles and the loftiest aims. The volume before us is beautifully bound, in a similar way to 'In the Snow,' by the same author, and is therefore very suitable for a present."—*Westminster Gazette.*

"A pleasing novelty in the style and character of the book, which is well and clearly sustained in the manner it is carried out."—*Northern Press.*

"Each stage furnishes the material for a dramatic scene; are very well hit off, and the whole makes up a graphic picture."—*Month.*

"'Clarewell' will give not only an hour of pleasant reading, but will, from the nature of the subject, be eminently suggestive of deep and important truths."—*Tablet.*

WORKS BY LADY GEORGIANA FULLERTON.

Life of Mary Fitzgerald, a Child of the Sacred Heart. Price 1s.; cloth extra, 2s.

BURNS, OATES, & CO., 63, PATERNOSTER ROW, E.C.

Rose Leblanc.   A Tale of great interest.
Cloth, 3s.

Grantley Manor.   (The well-known and favourite Novel).   Cloth, 3s.; cheap edition,
2s. 6d.

Life of St. Frances of Rome.   Neat cloth,
2s. 6d.; cheap edition, 1s. 8d.

Edited by the Same.

Our Lady's Little Books.   Neat cloth, 2s.;
separate Numbers, 4d. each.

Life of the Honourable E. Dormer, late of
the 60th Rifles.   1s.; cloth extra, 2s.

Helpers of the Holy Souls.   6d.

Tales from the Diary of a Sister of Mercy.
By C. M. BRAME.

CONTENTS : The Double Marriage—The Cross and
the Crown—The Novice—The Fatal Accident—The
Priest's Death—The Gambler's Wife—The Apostate
—The Besetting Sin.

Beautifully bound in bevelled cloth, 3s. 6d.

" Written in a chaste, simple, and touching style."—*Tablet.*
" This book is a casket; and those who open it will find the
gem within."—*Register.*
" Calculated to promote the spread of virtue, and to check that
of vice ; and cannot fail to have a good effect upon all—young
and old—into whose hands it may fall."—*Nation.*
" A neat volume, composed of agreeable and instructive tales.

Each of its tales concludes with a moral, which supplies food for reflection."—*Westminster Gazette.*

"They are well and cleverly told, and the volume is neatly got up."—*Month.*

"Very well told; all full of religious allusions and expressions."—*Star.*

"Very well written, and life-like—many very pathetic."—*Catholic Opinion.*

"An excellent work; reminds us forcibly of Father Price's 'Sick Calls.'"—*Universe.*

"A very interesting series of tales."—*Sun.*

By the Same.

Angels' Visits: A Series of Tales. With
Frontispiece and Vignette. 3s. 6d.

"The tone of the book is excellent, and it will certainly make itself a great favourite with the young."—*Month.*

"Beautiful collection of Angel Stories. All who may wish to give any dear children a book which speaks in tones suited to the sweet simplicity of their innocent young hearts about holy things cannot do better than send for 'Angels' Visits.'"—*Weekly Register.*

"One of the prettiest books for children we have seen."—*Tablet.*

"A book which excites more than ordinary praise. We have great satisfaction in recommending to parents and all who have the charge of children this charming volume."—*Northern Press.*

"A good present for children. An improvement on the 'Diary of a Sister of Mercy.'"—*Universe.*

"Touchingly written, and evidently the emanation of a refined and pious mind."—*Church Times.*

"A charming little book, full of beautiful stories of the family of angels."—*Church Opinion.*

"A nicely-written volume."—*Bookseller.*

"Gracefully-written stories."—*Star.*

Just out, ornamental cloth, 5s.

Legends of Our Lady and the Saints: or, Our
Children's Book of Stories in Verse. Written

for the Recitations of the Pupils of the Schools of the Holy Child Jesus, St. Leonards-on-Sea. Cheap Edition, 2s. 6d.

"It is a beautiful religious idea that is realised in the 'Legends of Our Lady and the Saints.' We are bound to add that it has been successfully carried out by the good nuns of St. Leonards. The children of their Schools are unusually favoured in having so much genius and taste exerted for their instruction and delight. The book is very daintily decorated and bound, and forms a charming present for pious children."—*Tablet.*

"The 'Legends' are so beautiful, that they ought to be read by all lovers of poetry."—*Bookseller.*

"Graceful poems."—*Month.*

Edith Sydney: a Tale of the Catholic Movement. By MISS OXENHAM. 5s.

"A novel for the novel-reader, and at the same time it is a guide to the convert and a help to their instructors."—*Universe.*

"Miss Oxenham shows herself to be a fair writer of a controversial tale, as well as a clever delineator of character."—*Tablet.*

"A charming romance. We introduce 'Edith Sydney' to our readers, confident that she will be a safe and welcome visitor in many a domestic circle, and will attain high favour with the Catholic reading public."—*Nation.*

"Miss Oxenham seems to possess considerable powers for the delineation of character and incident."—*Month.*

Not Yet: a Tale of the Present Time. By Miss OXENHAM. 5s.

"The lighter order of Catholic literature receives a very welcome addition in this story, which is original and very striking. The author is mistress of a style which is light and pleasant. The work is one to which we can give our heartiest commendation."—*Cork Examiner.*

"We are indebted to Miss Oxenham for one of the most interesting sensational Catholic tales yet published."—*Catholic Opinion.*

"Wholesome and pleasant reading, evincing a refined and cultivated understanding."—*Union Review.*

"Miss Oxenham's work would rank well even among Mudie's novels, although its one-volume form is likely to be unfavourable in the eyes of ordinary novel-readers ; but, in nine cases out of ten, a novelette is more effective than a regular novel, and any more padding would have merely diluted the vivid and unflagging interest which the authoress of 'Not Yet' has imparted to her elegantly-bound volume. The plot is as original as a plot can be ; it is well laid and carefully and ably worked out."—*Westminster Gazette.*

Nellie Netterville : a Tale of Ireland in the Time of Cromwell. By CECILIA CADDELL, Author of " Wild Times." 5s. ; cheap edition, 3s. 6d.

" A very interesting story. The author's style is pleasing, picturesque, and good, and we recommend our readers to obtain the book for themselves."—*Church News.*

" A tale well told and of great interest."—*Catholic Opinion.*

" Pretty pathetic story—well told."—*Star.*

" Pretty book-history of cruelties inflicted by Protestant domination in the sister country—full of stirring and affecting passages."—*Church Review.*

" Tale is well told, and many of the incidents, especially the burning of the chapel with the priest and congregation by the Cromwellian soldiers, are intensely interesting."—*Universe.*

" By a writer well known, whose reputation will certainly not suffer by her new production."—*Month.*

Marie ; or, the Workwoman of Liège. By CECILIA CADDELL. Cloth, 3s. 6d.

" This is another of those valuable works like that of ' Marie Eustelle Harpain.' Time would fail us were we to enumerate

either her marvellous acts of charity, or the heroic sufferings she
endured for the sake of others, or the wonderful revelations with
which her faith and charity were rewarded."—*Tablet.*

"The author of ' Wild Times,' and other favourite works, is
to be congratulated on the issue of a volume which is of more
service than any book of fiction, however stirring. It is a beautiful work—beautiful in its theme and in its execution."—*Weekly
Register.*

"Miss Caddell has given us a very interesting biography of
' Marie Sellier, the Workwoman of Liège,' known in the 17th
century as 'Sœur Marie Albert.' Examples such as that so grace-
fully set forth in this volume are much needed among us."—
Month.

The Countess of Glosswood: a Tale of the Times of the Stuarts. From the French. 3s. 6d.

"The tale is well written, and the translation seems cleverly
done."—*Month.*

"This volume is prettily got up, and we can strongly recommend it to all as an excellent and instructive little book to place
in the hands of the young."—*Westminster Gazette.*

"An excellent translation, and a very pretty tale, well told."
—*Catholic Opinion.*

"This is a pretty tale of a Puritan conversion in the time of
Charles II., prettily got up, and a pleasing addition to our
lending-libraries."—*Tablet.*

"This tale belongs to a class of which we have had to thank
Messrs. Burns for many beautiful specimens. Such books, while
they are delightful reading to us who are happily Catholics, have
another important merit—they set forth the claims of Catholicism,
and must do a vast deal of good among Protestants who casually
meet with and peruse them. The book before us is beautifully
got up, and would be an ornament to any table."—*Weekly Register.*

www.ingramcontent.com/pod-product-compliance
Lightning Source LLC
Chambersburg PA
CBHW030730280326
41926CB00086B/1060